PENGUIN BOOKS — GREAT FOOD

## The Joys of Excess

SAMUEL PEPYS (1633–1703) was a naval administrator and Member of Parliament, and is best remembered as a diarist. Kept between 1660 and 1669 and written in Shelton's shorthand, Pepys' diary recorded major historical events, like the Plague and the Great Fire of London, alongside his more personal concerns and activities, including politics, his work in public life and rows with his wife, Elizabeth. Throughout are his fascinating thoughts on food, including his first encounters with drinking chocolate.

D1322974

# The Joys of Excess

SAMUEL PEPYS

PENGUIN BOOKS

PENGUIN BOOKS

Published by the Penguin Group
Penguin Books Ltd, 80 Strand, London WC2R 0RL, England
Penguin Group (USA) Inc., 375 Hudson Street, New York, New York 10014, USA
Penguin Group (Canada), 90 Eglinton Avenue East, Suite 700, Toronto, Ontario,
Canada M4P 2Y3 (a division of Pearson Penguin Canada Inc.)
Penguin Ireland, 25 St Stephen's Green, Dublin 2, Ireland
(a division of Penguin Books Ltd)
Penguin Group (Australia), 250 Camberwell Road, Camberwell, Victoria 3124,
Australia (a division of Pearson Australia Group Pty Ltd)
Penguin Books India Pvt Ltd, 11 Community Centre,
Panchsheel Park, New Delhi – 110 017, India
Penguin Group (NZ), 67 Apollo Drive, Rosedale, Auckland 0632, New Zealand
(a division of Pearson New Zealand Ltd)
Penguin Books (South Africa) (Pty) Ltd, 24 Sturdee Avenue,
Rosebank, Johannesburg 2196, South Africa

Penguin Books Ltd, Registered Offices: 80 Strand, London WC2R 0RL, England

www.penguin.com

*The Shorter Pepys* first published 1985
This selection published in Penguin Books 2011
This edition published for The Book People Ltd, 2011
Hall Wood Avenue, Haydock, St Helens, WA11 9UL

1

Set in 10.75/13pt Berkeley Oldstyle Book
Typeset by Jouve (UK), Milton Keynes
Printed in Great Britain by Clays Ltd, St Ives plc

Cover design based on a pattern from a plate
from Brislington Pottery, *c.* 1662–85.
Tin-glazed earthenware with painted decoration.
(Photograph copyright © Victoria & Albert Museum.)
Picture research by Samantha Johnson. Lettering by Stephen Raw

ISBN 978–0–241–96080–6

www.greenpenguin.co.uk

Penguin Books is committed to a sustainable
future for our business, our readers and our
planet. This book is made from paper certified
by the Forest Stewardship Council.

# Contents

# 1660: Wine from the Rhine and a Cupp of China Tea

January 26.   Home from my office to my Lord's lodgings, where my wife had got ready a very fine dinner: *viz.* a dish of marrow-bones. A leg of mutton. A loin of veal. A dish of fowl, three pullets, and two dozen of larks, all in a dish. A great tart. A neat's tongue. A dish of anchoves. A dish of prawns, and cheese. My company was my father, my uncle Fenner, his two sons, Mr. Pierce, and all their wifes, and my brother Tom. We were as merry as I could frame myself to be in that company. W. Joyce, talking after the old rate and drinking hard, vexed his father and mother and wife. And I did perceive that Mrs. Pierce her coming so gallant, that it put the two young women quite out of courage. When it became dark, they all went away but Mr. Pierce and W. Joyce and their wifes and Tom, and drank a bottle of wine afterwards, so that Will did heartily anger his father and mother by staying. At which I and my wife were very much pleased. Then they all went and I fell to writing of two Characters for Mr. Downing, and carried them to him at 9 a-clock at night; and he did not like them but corrected them, so that tomorrow I am to do them anew. To my Lord's lodging again and sat by the great log, it being now a very good fire, with my wife; and eat a bit and so home.

28.   To Heaven; where Luellin and I dined on a breast of mutton all alone, discoursing of the changes that we have seen and the happiness of them that have estates of their own.

May 30.   About 8 a-clock in the morning, the Lieutenant came to me to know whether I would eat a dish of Mackrell, newly-ketched this morning, for my breakfast – which the Captain and we did in the coach. All yesterday and today I have a great deal of pain in making water and in my back, which made me afeared. But it proved nothing but cold which I took yesterday night.

August 9.   With Judge-Advocate Fowler, Mr. Creed and Mr. Sheply to the Rhenish winehouse, and Capt. Hayward of the *Plymouth*, who is now ordered to carry my Lord Winchelsea Embassador to Constantinople. We were very merry, and Judge-Advocate did give Capt. Hayward his oath of Allegiance and Supremacy. Thence to my office of Privy Seale; and having signed some things there, with Mr. Moore and Deane Fuller to the Leg in King street; and sending for my wife, we dined there – very merry, and after dinner parted. After dinner, with my wife to Mrs. Blackburne to visit her. She being within, I left my wife there; and I to the Privy Seal, where I despatch some business; and from thence to Mrs. Blackburne again, who did treat my wife and I with a great deal of civility and did give us a fine collation of collar of beef, &c. Thence, I having my head full of drink through having drunk so much Rhenish wine in the morning and more in the afternoon at Mrs. Blackburne. Came home and so to bed, not well; and very ill all night.

10.   I had a great deal of pain all night and a great looseness upon me, so that I could not sleep. In the morning I rose with much pain and to the office I went and dined at home; and after dinner, with great pain in my back, I went by water to Whitehall to the Privy Seale; and that done, with Mr. Moore and Creed to Hideparke by coach and saw a fine foot-race, three times round the park.

11.   I rose today without any pain, which makes me think that my pain yesterday was nothing but from my drinking too much the day before.

12.   *Lordsday*. To my Lord; and with him to Whitehall chapel, where Mr. Calamy preached and made a good sermon up[on] these words: 'To whom much is given, of him much is required.' He was very officious with his three reverences to the King, as others do. After sermon a brave Anthem of Capt. Cookes, which he himself sung, and the King was well pleased with it. My Lord dined at my Lord Chamberlins and I at his house with Mr. Sheply. After that I went to walk; and meeting Mrs. Lane of Westminster hall, I took her to my Lord's and did give her a bottle of wine in the garden, where Mr. Fairebrother of Cambridge did come and find us and drank with us. After that I took her to my house, where I was exceeding free in dallying with her, and she not unfree to take it. At night home and called at my father's, where I found Mr. Fairebrother; but I did not stay but went homewards and called in at Mr. Rawlinsons, whither my uncle Wight was coming; and did come, but was exceeding angry (he being a little fuddled, and I think it was that I should

3

see him in that case) as I never saw him in all my life – which I was somewhat troubled at. Home and to bed.

23. To the Admiralty chamber, where we and Mr. Coventry have a meeting about several businesses. Among others, it was moved that Phin. Pett (kinsman to the Commissioner) of Chatham should be suspended his imployment till he had answered to some articles put in against him; as, that he should formerly say that the King was a bastard and his mother a whore. Thence to Westminster hall, where I met with my father Bowyer and Mr. Spicer, and them I took to the Leg in King's street and did give them a dish or two of meat; and so away to the Privy Seale, where the King being out of Towne, we have had nothing to do these two days. To Westminster hall, where I met with W. Symons, T. Doling and Mr. Booth, and with them to the Dogg, where we eat a Muske millon (the first that I have eat this year) and were very merry with W. Symons, calling him Mr. Deane, because of the Deanes lands that his uncle had left him, which are like to be lost all. Thence home by water; and very late at night writing letters to my Lord to Hinchingbrooke and also to the Vice-Admirall in the Downes; and so to bed.

24. Office; and then with Sir W. Batten and Sir W. Penn to the parish church to find out a place where to build a seat or a gallery to sit in; and did find one, which is to be done speedily. Thence with them to dinner at a tavern in Thames street, where they were invited to a roasted haunch of vension and other very good victuals and company. Thence to Whitehall to the Privy Seale, but

nothing to do. At night by land to my father's, where I found my mother not very well. I did give her a pint of sack. My father came in and Dr. T. Pepys, who talked with me in French a great while about looking out of a place for him. But I find him a weak man and speaks the worst French that ever I heard of one that hath been so long beyond sea. Thence into Paul's churchyard and bought Barkley's *Argenis* in Latin; and so home and to bed. I find at home that Capt. Bun hath sent me four dozen bottles of wine to me today. The King came back to Whitehall tonight.

27.   This morning comes one with a vessel of North-downe ale from Mr. Pierce the purser to me. And after him, another with a brave Turkey carpet and a Jarre of Olives from Capt. Cuttance and a pair of fine Turtle-doves from John Burr to my wife. These things came up today in our smack; and my boy Ely came along with them and came after office was done to see me. I did give him half a crowne because I saw that he was ready to cry to see that he could not be entertained by me here. In the afternoon to the Privy Seale, where good stir of work now toward the end of the month. From thence with Mr. Mount, Luellin and others to the Bullhead till late, and so home. Where about 10 a-clock Maj. Hart came to me – whom I did receive with wine and a dish of Anchoves, which made me so dry that I was ill with them all night and was fain to have the girl rise to fetch me some drink.

September 21.   Back by water about 8 a-clock; and upon the water saw [the] corps of the Duke of Gloucester brought down Somersett house stairs to go by water to

Westminster to be buried tonight. I landed at the old Swan and went to the Hoope taverne and (by former agreement) sent for Mr. Chaplin, who with Nich. Osborne and one Daniel came to us and there we drank off two or three quarts of wine, which was very good (the drawing of our wine causing a great quarrell in the house between the two drawers which should draw us the best). Home, where I find my boy (my mayd's brother) come out of the country today; but was gone to bed and so I could not see him tonight. I to bed.

22. This morning I called up the boy to me and find him a pretty well-looked boy, and one that I think will please me. I went this morning to Westminster by land along with Luellin. We walked on to Fleetstreete, where at Mr. Standings in Salsbury court we drank our morning draught and had a pickled herring. Among other discourse here, he told me how the pretty woman that I always loved at the beginning of Cheapeside that sells children's coates was served by the Lady Bennett (a famous Strumpet), who by counterfeiting to fall into a swoune upon the sight of her in her shop, became acquainted with her and at last got her ends of her to lie with a gallant that had hired her to Procure this poor soul for him. To Westminster to my Lord's; and there in the house of office vomited up all my breakfast, my stomach being ill all this day by reason of the last night's debauch.

25. To the office, where Sir W. Batten, Coll. Slingsby, and I sat a while; and Sir R. Ford coming to us about some business, we talked together of the interest of this kingdom to have a peace with Spain and a war with

France and Holland – where Sir R. Ford talked like a man of great reason and experience. And afterwards did send for a Cupp of Tee (a China drink of which I never had drank before) and went away. Then came Coll. Birch and Sir R. Browne (by a former appointment) and with them from Towre wharf in the barge belonging to our office we went to Deptford to pay off the ship.

28. *office day*. All the afternoon at home among my workmen; work till 10 or 11 at night; and did give them drink and were very merry with them – it being my luck to meet with a sort of Drolling workmen upon all occasions. To bed.

29. All day at home to make an end of our dirty work of the playsterers; and indeed, my Kitchin is now so handsome that I did not repent of all the trouble that I have been put to to have it done. This day or yesterday I hear Prince Robt is come to Court; but welcome to nobody.

October 11. In the morning to my Lord's, where I met with Mr. Creed, and with him and Mr. Blackburne to the Rhenish winehouse – where we sat drinking of healths a great while, a thing which Mr. Blackburne formerly would not upon any terms have done. After we had done there, Mr. Creed and I to the Leg in King street to dinner, where he and I and my Will had a good udder to dinner; and from thence to walk in St. James's Park – where we observed the several engines at work to draw up water, with which sight I was very much pleased. Here in the park we met with Mr. Salsbury, who took Mr. Creed and me to the Cockpitt to see *The Moore of Venice*, which was well done. Burt acted the Moore; by the same token, a very pretty lady that sot by me cried to see Desdimona smothered.

13. To my Lord's in the morning, where I met with Capt. Cuttance. But my Lord not being up, I went out to Charing cross to see Maj.-Gen. Harrison hanged, drawn, and quartered – which was done there – he looking as cheerfully as any man could do in that condition. He was presently cut down and his head and his heart shown to the people, at which there was great shouts of joy. It is said that he said that he was sure to come shortly at the right hand of Christ to judge them that now have judged him. And that his wife doth expect his coming again. Thus it was my chance to see the King beheaded at Whitehall and to see the first blood shed in revenge for the blood of the King at Charing cross. From thence to my Lord's and took Capt. Cuttance and Mr. Sheply to the Sun taverne and did give them some oysters.

17. *office day*. At noon comes Mr. Creede to me, whom I took along with me to the feathers in Fishstreete, where I was invited by Capt. Cuttance to dinner – a dinner made by Mr. Dawes and his brother. We have two or three dishes of meat well done. Their great designe was to get me concerned in a business of theirs about a vessel of theirs that is in the service, hired by the King, in which I promise to do them all the service I can.

22. *office day*. After that to dinner at home upon some ribbs of roast beef from the Cookes (which of late we have been forced to do because of our house being alway

under the painters' and other people's hands, that we could not dress it ourselfs): after dinner to my Lord's, where I find all preparing for my Lord's going to sea to fetch the Queene tomorrow. At night my Lord came home, with whom I stayed long and talked of many things. Among others, I got leave of him to have his picture, that was done by Lilly, coppyed.

November 30.  *Office day*. To the office in the morning, where Sir G. Carter[e]t did give us an account how Mr. Holland doth entend to prevail with the parliament that his project of discharging the seamen all at present by tickett and so to promise interest to all men that will lend money upon them at 8 per cent for so long as they are unpaid – whereby he doth think to take away the growing debt, which doth now lie upon the kingdom for lack of present money to discharge the seamen. But this we are troubled at, as some diminucion to us. I having two barrells of Oysters at home, I caused one of them and some wine to be brought to the inner room in the office, and there the Principal Officers did go and eat them. So we sat till noon; and then to dinner. And to it again in the afternoon till night. At home I sent for Mr. Hater and broke the other barrell with him. And did afterward sit down, discoursing of sea tearmes to learn of him. And he being gone, I went up and sat till 12 at night again to make an end of my Lord's accounts – as I did the last night. Which at last I made a good end of; and so to bed.

December 13.  All the day long looking upon my workmen, who this day begin to paint my Parlour. Only at noon my Lady Batten and my wife came home, and so I step to my Lady's, where was Sir John Lawson and Capt. Holmes; and there we dined and had very good red wine of my Lady's own making in England.

21.   To my Lady and dined with her. She told me how dangerously ill the Princess Royall is: and that this morning she was said to be dead. That she hears that she hath married herself to young Jermin, which is worse then the Duke of Yorkes marrying the Chancellor's daughter – which is now publicly owned. After dinner to the office all the afternoon. At seven at night I walked through the dirt to Whitehall to see whether my Lord be come to town; and I find him come – and at supper; and I supped with him. He tells me that my aunt at Brampton hath voided a great Stone (the first time that ever I heard she was troubled therewith) and cannot possibly live long. That my uncle is pretty well, but full of pain still. After supper home and to bed.

22.   All the morning with my paynters – who will make an end of all this day, I hope. At noon I went to the Sun tavern on Fish streete hill to a dinner of Capt. Teddimans, where was my Lord Inchiquin (who seems to be a very fine person), Sir W. Pen, Capt. Cuttance, and one Mr. Lawrence (a fine gentleman now going to Algier) and other good company; where we have a very fine dinner, good Musique and a great deal of Wine. We stayed here very late; at last, Sir W. Pen and I home together, he so overgone with wine that he could hardly go; I was forced to lead him through the street and he was in a very merry and kind moode. I home (found my house clear of the

workmen and their work ended), my head troubled with wine; and I, very merry, went to bed – my head akeing all night.

25.   *Christmas day*. In the morning to church; where Mr. Mills made a very good sermon. After that home to dinner, where my wife and I and my brother Tom (who this morning came to see my wife's new mantle put on, which doth please me very well) – to a good shoulder of Mutton and a Chicken. After dinner to church again, my wife and I, where we have a dull sermon of a stranger which made me sleep; and so home; and I, before and after supper, to my Lute and Fullers *History*, at which I stayed all alone in my Chamber till 12 at night; and so to bed.

27.   With my wife to Sir W. Batten's to dinner, where much and good company. Good and much entertainment. My wife, not very well, went home. I stayed late there, seeing them play at cards; and so home and to bed. This afternoon there came in a strange lord to Sir W. Batten's by a mistake and enters discourse with him, so that we could not be rid of him till Sir Arn. Brames and Mr. Bens and Sir Wm. fell a-drinking to him till he was drunk, and so sent him away. About the middle of the night I was very ill, I think with eating and drinking too much; and so I was forced to call the mayde (who pleased my wife and I in her running up and down so inocently in her smock) and vomited in the bason; and so to sleep, and in the morning was pretty well – only got cold and so have pain in pissing, as I used to have.

# 1661: Botargo, Bread and Butter by Moonshine

January 1. Comes in my Brother Tho., and after him my father, Dr. Tho. Pepys, my uncle Fenner and his two sons (Anthonys only child dying this morning, yet he was so civil to come and was pretty merry) to breakfast. And I have for them a barrel of oysters, a dish of neat's tongues, and a dish of Anchoves – wine of all sorts, and Northdown ale. We were very merry till about 11 a-clock, and then they went away. At noon I carried my wife by Coach to my Cosen Tho. Pepys; where we, with my father, Dr. Tho., Cozen Stradwick, Scott, and their wifes dined. Here I saw first his Second wife, which is a very respectful woman. But his dinner a sorry, poor dinner for a man of his estate – there being nothing but ordinary meat in it.

2. To my office, and there all the morning; and so home to dinner – where I found Pall (my sister) was come; but I do not let her sit down at table with me; which I do at first, that she may not expect it hereafter from me. After dinner I to Westminster by water – and there found my Brother Spicer at the Legg with all the rest of the Exchequer men (most of whom I now do not know) at dinner. I took a turne in the hall, and bought the King and Chancellors speeches at the dissolving the parliament last Saturday. This day I lent Sir W. Batten and Capt. Rider my

chine of beef for to serve at dinner tomorrow at Trinity house, the Duke of Albemarle being to be there and all the rest of the Bretheren, it being a great day for the reading over of their new Charter which the King hath newly given them.

3.  Early in the morning to the Exchequer, where I told over what money I have of my Lord's and my own there, which I find to be 970*l*: thence to Will's, where Spicer and I eat our dinner of a roasted leg of porke which Will did give us. And after that, I to the Theatre, where was acted *Beggars bush* – it being very well done; and here the first time that ever I saw Women come upon the stage. From thence to my father's, where I find my mother gone by Bird the carrier to Brampton, upon my uncles great desire, my aunt being now in despair of life. So home.

February 24  *Sunday*. Mr. Mills made an excellent sermon in the morning against Drunkennesse that ever I heard in my life. I dined at home. Another good one of his in the afternoon. My Valentine had her fine gloves on at church today that I did give her. After sermon my wife and I into Sir W. Batten's and sat awhile. Then home – I to read. Then to supper and to bed.

26.  *Shrovetuesday*. I left my wife in bed, being indisposed by reason of *ceux-là* – and I to Mrs. Turners, who I find busy with The[oph]. and Joyce making of things ready for Fritters. So I to Mr. Crews and there delivered Cottgraves dictionary – to my Lady Jemimah. And then with Mr. Moore to my Cozen Tom Pepys's; but he being out of town, I spoke with his lady – though not of the business

I went about, which was to borrow 1000*l* for my Lord. Back to Mrs. Turners, where several friends, all strangers to me but Mr. Armiger, din'd. Very merry, and the best fritters that ever I eat in my life. After that look out at Window; saw the flinging at Cocks.

27.   At the office all the morning. Then came into the garden to me young Mr. Powell and Mr. Hooke, that I once knew at Cambridge, and I took them in and gave them a bottle of wine and so parted. Then I called for a dish of fish, which we had for dinner – this being the first day of Lent; and I do entend to try whether I can keep it or no. This day the Commissioners of Parliament begin to pay off the Fleet, beginning with the *Hampshire* – and do it at Guildhall for fear of going out of the town into the power of the seamen, who are highly incensed against them.

April 23.   *Coronacion day*. Here I stayed walking up and down; and at last, upon one of the side-stalls, I stood and saw the King come in with all the persons (but the Souldiers) that were yesterday in the cavalcade; and a most pleasant sight it was to see them in their several robes. And the King came in with his Crowne on and his sceptre in his hand – under a Canopy borne up by six silver staves, carried by Barons of the Cinqueports – and little bells at every end. And after a long time he got up to the farther end, and all set themselfs down at their several tables – and that was also a rare sight. And the King's first Course carried up by the Knights of the bath. And many fine ceremonies there was of the Heralds leading up people before him and bowing; and my Lord of Albimarles going to the Kitchin and eat a bit of the first dish that was to go to the King's table. But above all was these three Lords, Northumberland and Suffolke and Duke of Ormond, coming before the Courses on horseback and staying so all dinner-time; and at last, to bring up (Dymock) the King's Champion, all in armor on horseback, with his Speare and targett carried before him. And a herald proclaim that if any dare deny Ch. Steward to be lawful King of England, here was a Champion that would fight with him; and with those words the Champion flings down his gantlet; and all this he doth three times in his going up toward the King's table. At last, when he is come, the King Drinkes to him and then sends him the Cup, which is of gold; and he drinks it off and then rides back again with the cup in his hand. I went from table to table to see the Bishops and all others at their dinner, and was infinite pleased with it. And at the Lords' table I met with Wll. Howe and he spoke to my Lord for me and he did give him four rabbits and a pullet; and so I got it, and Mr. Creed and I got Mr. Michell to give us some bread and so we at a Stall eat it, as everybody else did what they could get. I took a great deal of pleasure to go up and down and look upon the ladies – and to hear the Musique of all sorts; but above all, the 24 viollins. And strange it is, to think that these two days have held up fair till now that all is done and the King gone out of the hall; and then it fell a-raining and thundering and lightening as I have not seen it do some years – which people did take great notice of God's blessing of the work of these two days – which is a foolery, to take too much notice of such things.

15

[To] Mr. Bowyers, [where] a great deal of company; some I knew, others I did not. Here we stayed upon the leads and below till it was late, expecting to see the Fireworkes; but they were not performd tonight. Only, the City had a light like a glory round about it, with bonefyres. To Axe yard, in which, at the further end, there was three great bonefyres and a great many great gallants, men and women; and they laid hold of us and would have us drink the King's health upon our knee, kneeling upon a fagott; which we all did, they drinking to us one after another – which we thought a strange Frolique. But these gallants continued thus a great while, and I wondered to see how the ladies did tiple. At last I sent my wife and her bedfellow to bed, and Mr. Hunt and I went in with Mr. Thornbury (who did give the company all their wines, he being yeoman of the wine-cellar to the King) to his house; and there we drank the King's health and nothing else, till one of the genlemen fell down stark drunk and there lay speweing. And I went to my Lord's pretty well. But no sooner a-bed with Mr. Sheply but my head begun to turne and I to vomitt, and if ever I was foxed it was now – which I cannot say yet, because I fell asleep and sleep till morning – only, when I waked I found myself wet with my spewing. Thus did the day end, with joy everywhere.

24.   Waked in the morning with my head in a sad taking through the last night's drink, which I am very sorry for. So rise and went out with Mr. Creed to drink our morning draught, which he did give me in Chocolate to settle my stomach.

May 14.   In the evening Mr. Sheply came to me for some money; and so he and I to the Mitre and there we had good wine and a gammon of bacon. My Uncle Wight, Mr. Talbott, and others were with us, and we were pretty merry. So at night home and to bed – finding my head grow weak nowadays if I come to drink wine; and therefore hope that I shall leave it off of myself, which I pray God I could do.

June 5.   After dinner to the office, where we sat and did business; and then Sir W. Penn and I went home with Sir R. Slingsby to bowles in his ally and there had good sport; and afterward went in and drank and talked. So home, Sir William and I; and it being very hot weather, I took my flagilette and played upon the leads in the garden, where Sir W. Penn came out in his shirt into his leads and there we stayed talking and singing and drinking of great draughts of Clarret and eating botargo and bread and butter till 12 at night, it being moonshine. And so to bed – very near fuddled.

6.   My head hath aked all night and all this morning with my last night's debauch. Called up this morning by Lieut. Lambert, who is now made Captain of the *Norwich*; and he and I went down by water to Greenwich, in our way observing and discoursing upon the things of a ship; he telling me all I asked him – which was of good use to me. There we went and eat and drank and hear musique at the Globe; and saw the simple motion that is there, of a woman with a rod in her hand, keeping time to the music while it plays – which is simple methinks.

September 9.　To the Privy Seale in the morning, but my Lord did not come. So I went with Capt. Morrice at his desire into the King's Privy Kitchin to Mr. Sayres the Master-Cooke, and there we had a good slice of beef or two to our breakfast. And from thence he took us into the wine-cellar; where by my troth we were very merry, and I drank too much wine – and all along had great and perticular kindness from Mr. Sayre. But I drank so much wine that I was not fit for business; and therefore, at noon I went and walked in Westminster hall a while; and thence to Salsbury Court playhouse, where was acted the first time *Tis pitty shee's a Whore* – a simple play and ill acted; only, it was my fortune to sit by a most pretty and most ingenious lady, which pleased me much.

29.　*Lords day*. At dinner and supper, I drank, I know not how, of my owne accord, so much wine, that I was even almost foxed and my head aked all night. So home, and to bed without prayers, which I never did yet since I came to the house of a Sonday night: I being now so out of order that I durst not read prayers, for fear of being perceived by my servants in what case I was. So to bed.

October 5.　At the office all the morning; then dined at home, and so stayed at home all the afternoon, putting up my Lord's Modell of the *Royall James*, which I borrowed of him long ago to hang up in my room. And at night Sir W. Pen and I alone to the Dolphin and there eat some bloat-herrings and drank good sack. Then came in Sir W. Warren and another and stayed a while with us; and then Sir Arnld. Brames, with whom we stayed late and till we had drank too much wine; so home and I to bed, pleased at my afternoon's work in hanging up the Shipp. So to bed.

17.    To the cook's, and there dined with Capt. Lambert and had much talk of Portugall from whence he is lately come, and he tells me that it is a very poor dirty place – I mean the City and Court of Lisbone. That the King is a very rude and simple fellow; and for reviling of somebody a little while ago and calling of him cuckold, was run into the cods with a sword, and had been killed had he not told them that he was their king. That there is there no glass windows, nor will have any. That the King hath his meat sent up by a dozen of lazy guards, and in pipkins sometimes, to his own table – and sometimes nothing but fruits, and now and then half a hen. And that now the Infanta is becoming our Queene, she is come to have a whole hen or goose to her table – which is not ordinary.

19.    At the office all morning; and at noon Mr. Coventry, who sat with us all this morning, and Sir G. Carteret, Sir W. Penn and myself by coach to Capt. Marshes at Limehouse, to a house that hath been their ancestors for this 250 years – close by the Limehouse which gives the name to the place. Here they have a design to get the King to hire a docke for the herring busses (which is now the great design on foote) to lie up in. We had a very good and handsome dinner, and excellent wine.

November 3.    *Lords day*. This day I stirred not out, but took physique and it did work very well; and all the day, as I was at leisure, I did read in Fuller's *Holy Warr* (which

I have of late bought) and did try to make a Song in the prayse of a Liberall genius (as I take my own to be) to all studies and pleasures; but it not proving to my mind, I did reject it and so proceeded not in it. At night my wife and I had a good supper by ourselfs, of a pullet hashed; which pleased me much to see my condition come to allow ourselfs a dish like that. And so at night to bed.

4. In the morning, being very rainy, by Coach with Sir W. Penn and my wife to Whitehall; and sent her to Mrs. Hunts, and he and I to Mr. Coventry about business; and so sent for her again, and all three home again; only, I to the Miter (Mr. Rawlinson's), where Mr. Pierce the purser had got us a most rare Chine of beef and a dish of marrow bones.

25. To Westminster hall in the morning with Capt. Lambert – and there he did at the Dogg give me, and some other friends of his, his foy, he being to set sail today toward the Streights. Here we had oysters and good wine. Having this morning met in the hall with Mr. Sanchy, we appointed to meet at the play this afternoon. At noon, at the rising of the House, I met with Sir W. Pen, and with him and Maj.-Gen. Massy (who I find by discourse to be a very ingenious man, and among other things, a great master in the Secresys of powder and fire-workes) and another Knight to dinner at the Swan in the Palace yard, and our meat brought from the Legg. And after dinner Sir W. Pen and I to the Theatre and there saw *The Country Captain*, a dull play; and that being done, I left him with his Torys and went to the Opera and saw the last act of *The Bondman*; and there find Mr. Sanchy

and Mrs. Mary Archer, sister to the fair Betty, whom I did admire at Cambrige. And thence took them to the fleece in Covent Garden, there to bid good-night to Sir W. Penn, who stayed for me. But Mr. Sanchy could not by any argument get his lady to trust herself with him into the taverne, which he was much troubled at; and so we returned immediately into the city by Coach, and at the Miter in Cheapside there light and drank, and then set her at her uncles in the Old Jury. And so he and I back again thither and drank till past 12 at night, till I had drank something too much – he all the while telling me his intentions to get this girle, who is worth 1000*l*.

December 1. *Lords day*. We have this day cut a brave Coller of Brawne from Winchcombe, which proves very good. And also opened the glass of Girkins which Capt. Cock did give my wife the other day, which are rare things. So at night to bed.

22. *Lords day*. To church in the morning, where the Reader made a boyish young sermon. Home to dinner; and there I took occasion, from the blackness of the meat as it came out of the pot, to fall out with my wife and the maids for their sluttery; and so left the table and went up to read in Mr. Selden till church time.

26. This morning Sir W. Pen and I to the Treasury office; and there we paid off the *Amity* and another ship, and so home; and after dinner Sir Wm. came to me, and he and his son and daughter and I and my wife by Coach to Moorefields to walk (but it was most foule weather); and so we went into an alehouse and there eat some cakes and

ale; and a Washeall-bowle woman and girl came to us and sung to us; and after all was done, I called my boy (Waynman) to us to eat some cake that was left, and the woman of the house told us that he had called for two Cakes and a pot of ale for himself, at which I was angry and am resolved to correct him for it. So home; and Sir W. Penn and his son and daughter to supper to me to a good Turkey, and were merry at Cards; and so to bed.

30.   At the office about this Estimate. And so with my wife and Sir. W. Penn to see our pictures – which do not much displease us. And so back again; and I stayed at the Miter, whither I had invited all my old acquaintance of the Exchequer to a good Chine of beefe – which with three barrels of oysters and three pullets and plenty of wine and mirth, was our dinner. There was about twelve of us.

# 1662: Boiled Great Oysters and a Brace of Stewed Carps

January 15. This morning Mr. Berchenshaw came again; and after he had examined me and taught me something in my work, he and I went to breakfast in my chamber, upon a Coller of brawne. And after we had eaten, he asked me whether we have not committed a fault in eating today, telling me that it is a fast-day, ordered by the parliament to pray for more seasonable weather – it having hitherto been some summer weather, that it is, both as to warmth and every other thing, just as if it were the middle of May or June, which doth threaten a plague (as all men think) to fallow; for so it was almost the last winter and the whole year after hath been a very sickly time, to this day. I did not stir out of my house all day, but con'd my Musique; and at night, after supper to bed.

20. This morning Sir Wm. Batten and Penn and [I] did begin the examining the Treasurers accounts – the first that ever he hath passed in the office. Which is very long – and we were all at it till noon. Then to dinner, he providing a fine dinner for us; and we eate it at Sir Wm. Batten's, where we were very merry, there being at table the Treasurer and we three – Mr. Wayth, Fenn, Smith, Turner, and Mr Morrice the Wine Cooper (who this day did divide the two butts, which we four did send for, of Sherry from Cales, and mine was put into a hogshead and the vessell

filled up with four gallons of Malago wine; but what it will stand us in I know not, but it is the first great Quantity of wine that I ever bought). And after dinner to the office all the afternoon, till late at night. And then home, where my aunt and uncle Wight and Mrs. Anne Wight came to play at Cards (at gleeke, which she taught me and my wife the last week); and so to supper and then to Cards, and so good-night. Then I to my practice of Musique and then at 12 a-clock to bed. This day the workmen begin to make me a sellar door out of the back yard – which will much please me.

25.    At home and the office all the morning. Walking in the garden to give the gardener directions what to do this year (for I entend to have the garden handsome), Sir Wm. Pen came to me. Thence with him to the Trinity house to dinner, where Sir Richard Brown (one of the clerks of the Council, and who is much concerned against Sir N. Crisp's project of making a great sasse in the King's Lands about Deptford, to be a wett dock to hold 200 sail of ships – but the ground, it seems, was long since given by the King to Sir Richd.) was; and after the Trinity house men had done their business, the maister, Sir Wm. Rider, came to bid us welcome; and so to dinner – where good cheer and discourse, but I eat a little too much beef, which made me sick; and so after dinner we went to the office, and there in the garden I went in the darke and vomited, whereby I did much ease my stomach. Thence to supper with my wife to Sir Wm. Pens. And so while we were at supper, comes Mr. Moore with letters from my Lord Sandwich, speaking

of his lying still at Tanger, looking for the fleet – which we hope is now in a good way thither.

February 3.    After musique practice I went to the office, and there with the two Sir Wms all the morning about business. At noon I dined with Sir W. Batten with many friends more, it being his Wedding-day. And among other Froliques, it being their third year, they had three pyes, whereof the middlemost was made of an ovall form in an Ovall hole within the other two which made much mirth and was called the middle peace; and above all the rest, we had great striving to steal a spoonefull out of it; and I remember Mrs. Mills the minister's wife did steal one for me and did give it me; and to end all, Mrs. Shippman did fill the pie full of White wine (it holding at least a pint and a half) and did drink it off for a health to Sir Wm. and my Lady, it being the greatest draught that ever I did see a woman drink in my life. Before we had dined came Sir G. Carteret, and we went all three to the office and did business there till night. And then to Sir Wm. Batten again, and I went along with my Lady and the rest of the gentlewomen to Maj. Holmes's, and there we had a fine supper; among others, excellent lobsters, which I never eat at this time of the year before. The Major hath good lodgings at the Trinity house. Here we stayed late, and at last home. And being in my chamber, we do hear great noise of mirth at Sir Wm. Battens, tearing the ribbands from my Lady and him. So I to bed.

March 23.    *Lords day*. This morning was brought me my boyes fine livery, which is very handsome, and I do think to keep to black and gold lace upon gray, being the colour of my armes, for ever. To church in the morning. And so home with Sir W. Batten and there eat some boiled great oysters; and so home, and while I was at dinner with my wife, I was sick and was forced to vomitt up my oysters again and then I was well. To Whitehall and there met with Capt. Isham, this day come from Lisbone with letters from the Queene to the King. And did give me letters which speak that our fleet is all at Lisbon; and that the Queene doth not entend to embarque sooner then tomorrow come fortnight.

24. earely, Sir G. Carteret, both Sir Wms, and I on board the *Experiment* to dispatch her away, she being to carry things to the Maderas with the East India fleet. Here (Sir W. Penn going to Deptford to send more hands), we stayed till noon, talking and eating and drinking a good ham of English bacon; and having put things in good order, home – where I find Jane, my old maid, come out of the country; and I have a mind to have her again. By and by comes *la Belle* Perce to see my wife and to bring her a pair of peruques of hair, as the fashion now is for ladies to wear – which are pretty and are of my wife's own hair, or else I should not endure them. After a good while stay, I went to see if any play was acted, and I find none upon the post, it being passion weeke. To Westminster hall and there bought Mr. Grant's book of observations upon the weekly bills of Mortality – which appear to me, upon first sight, to be very pretty. So back again and took my wife, calling at my brother Tom's, whom I find full of work, which I am glad of; and thence at the New Exchange and so home. And I to Sir W. Battens and

supped there, out of pure hunger to save getting anything ready at home, which is a thing I do not nor shall
not use to do. So home and to bed.

26.   Up earely – this being, by God's great blessing, the
fourth solemne day of my cutting for the stone this day
four year. And am by God's mercy in very good health,
and like to do well, the Lord's name be praised for it.
To the office and Sir G. Carterets all the morning, about
business. At noon came my good guest[s] Madame
Turner, The[oph]., and Cosen Norton, and a gentleman,
one Mr. Lewin of the King's life-guard; by the same token
he told us of one of his fellows, killed this morning in
the dewell. I had a pretty dinner for them – *viz*: a brace
of stewed Carps, six roasted chicken, and a Jowle of
salmon hot, for the first course – a Tanzy and two neats'
tongues and cheese the second. And were very merry all
the afternoon, talking and singing and piping on the
Flagelette. In the evening they went with great pleasure
away; and I with great content, and my wife, walked half
an houre in the garden; and so home to supper and to
bed. We had a man-cook to dress dinner today, and sent
for Jane to help us. And my wife and she agreed 3*l* a year
(she would not serve under) till both could be better
provided; and so she stays with us.

30.   *Easterday*. Having my old black suit new-furbished,
I was pretty neat in clothes today – and my boy, his old
suit new-trimmed, very handsome. To church in the
morning. We had a lobster to supper with a crab Pegg
Pen sent my wife this afternoon; the reason of which we
cannot think, but something there is of plot or design

in it – for we have a little while carried ourselfs pretty strange to them. After supper, to bed.

April 1.   After dinner I and the two young ladies and my wife to the playhouse, the Opera, and saw *The Mayd in the mill*, a pretty good play [. . .] And that being done, in their coach I took them to Islington; and there, after a walk in the fields, I took them to the great Chescake house and entertained them, and so home; and after an hour stay with my Lady, their coach carried us home; and so, weary to bed.

22.   After taking leave of my wife, which we could hardly do kindly, because of her mind to go along with me – Sir W. Penn and I took coach and so over the bridge to Lambeth – W. Bodham and Tom Hewet going as clerks to Sir W. Penn, and my Will for me. Here we got a dish of buttered eggs, and there stayed till Sir G. Carteret came to us from Whitehall, who brought Dr. Clerke with him, at which I was very glad. And so we set out. And I was very much pleased with his company, and were very merry all the way.

25.   All the morning at Portsmouth at the pay; and then to dinner and again to the pay; and at night got the Doctor to go lie with me, and much pleased with his company; but I was much troubled in my eyes, by reason of the healths I have this day been forced to drink.

May 11.   *Lordsday*. To our own church in the morning; where our Minister being out of town, a dull, flat Presbiter preached. Dined at home, and my wife's brother with us, we having a good dish of stewed beef of Janes own dressing, which was well done, and a piece of Sturgeon, of a barrel lately sent me by Capt. Cocke. In the afternoon to Whitehall and there walked an hour or two in the parke, where I saw the King now out of mourning – in a suit laced with gold and silver, which it was said was out of fashion. Thence to the Wardrobe and there consulted with the ladies about our going to Hampton court tomorrow; and thence home and after settled business there, my wife and I to the Wardrobe; and there we lay all night in Capt. Ferrers chamber, but the bed so saft that I could not sleep that hot night.

25. *Lords day*. To trimming myself, which I have this week done every morning, with a pumice stone, which I learnt of Mr. Marsh when I was last at Portsmouth; and I find it very easy, speedy and cleanly, and shall continue the practice of it. To church and heard a good sermon of Mr. Woodcockes at our church. Dined at home, and Mr. Creede with me. This day I had the first dish of pease I have had this year.

29. With my wife and the two maids and the boy took boat and to Foxhall – where I have not been a great while – to the Old Spring garden [. . .] And so to another house that was an ordinary house, and here we have cakes and powdered beef and ale; and so home again by water, with much pleasure. This day, being the Kings birthday, was very solemnely observed; and the more for that the Queene this day comes to Hampton Court. In the evening bonefires were made, but nothing to the great number that was heretofore at the burning of the Rump. So to bed.

June 26.   Up and took phisique, but such as to go abroad with, only to loosen me, for I am bound. So to the office – and there all the morning, setting till noon; and then took Commissioner Pett home with me to dinner, where my stomach was turned when my sturgeon came to table, upon which I saw very many little worms creeping, which I suppose was through the staleness of the pickle. He being gone, comes Mr. Nicholson, my old fellow-student at Magdalen, and we played three or four things upon violin and Basse; and so parted, and I to my office till night; and then came Mr. Sheply and Creede in order to setting some accounts of my Lord right; and so to bed.

October 24.   After with great pleasure lying a great while, talking and sporting in bed with my wife (for we have [been] for some years now, and at present more and more, a very happy couple, blessed be God), I got up and to my office; and having done there some business, and by water and then walked to Deptford to discourse with Mr. Cowly and Davis about my late conceptions about keeping books of the distinct works done in the yards, against which I find no objection but their ignorance and unwillingness to do anything of pains and what is out of their old dull road. But I like it well, and will proceed in it. So home and dined there with my wife upon a most excellent dish of tripes of my own directing, covered with mustard, as I have heretofore seen them done at my Lord Crews; of which I made a very great meal and sent for a glass of wine for myself.

December 24.   This evening Mr. Gauden sent me, against Christmas, a great Chine of beefe and three dozen of Toungs. I did give 5*s*. to the man that brought it and half-crown to the porters. This day also, the parish Clerke brought the general bill of Mortality, which cost me half-Crowne more.

25. *Christmas day* [. . .] I walked home again with great pleasure; and there dined by my wife's bedside with great content, having a mess of brave plum-porridge and a roasted Pullett for dinner; and I sent for a mince-pie abroad, my wife not being well to make any herself yet. After dinner sat talking a good while with her, her [pain] being become less, and then to see Sir W. Penn a little; and so to my office, practising arithmetique alone with great content, till 11 at night; and so home to supper and to bed.

26. Up. My wife to the making of Christmas-pies all day, being now pretty well again. And I abroad to several places about small businesses; among others, bought a bake pan in Newgate market and sent it home; it cost me 16*s*. Then to [Mr. Moore at] the Wardrobe, who is not yet well. Hither came Mr. Battersby; and we falling into a discourse of a new book of Drollery in verse called *Hudebras*, I would needs go find it out; and met with it at the Temple, cost me 2*s*.- 6*d*. But when I came to read it, it is so silly an abuse of the Presbyter-Knight going to the warrs, that I am ashamed of it; and by and by meeting at Mr. Townsends at dinner, I sold it to him for 18*d*.

# 1663: Eeles, Teales and a Hot Umble-pie

January 13.   So my poor wife rose by 5 a-clock in the morning, before day, and went to market and bought fowle and many other things for dinner – with which I was highly pleased. And the chine of beef was done also before 6 a-clock, and my own Jacke, of which I was doubtful, doth carry it very well. Things being put in order and the Cooke come, I went to the office, where we sat till noon; and then broke up and I home – whither by and by comes Dr. Clerke and his lady – his sister and a she-Cosen, and Mr. Pierce and his wife, which was all my guest[s]. I had for them, after oysters – at first course, a hash of rabbits and lamb, and a rare chine of beef – next, a great dish of roasted fowl, cost me about 30s., and a tart; and then fruit and cheese. My dinner was noble and enough. I had my house mighty clean and neat, my room below with a good fire in it – my dining-room above, and my chamber being made a withdrawing-chamber, and my wife's a good fire also. I find my new table very proper, and will hold nine or ten people well, but eight with great room. After dinner, the women to Cards in my wife's chamber and the Doctor [and] Mr. Pierce in mine, because the dining-room smokes unless I keep a good charcole fire, which I was not then provided with. At night to supper; had a good sack-posset and cold meat and sent my guests away about 10 a-clock at night –

both them and myself highly pleased with our management of this day. And indeed, their company was very fine and Mrs. Clerke a very witty, fine lady, though a little conceited and proud. So weary to bed. I believe this day's feast will cost me near 5*l*.

15. Up, and to my office preparing things. By and by we met and sat, Mr. Coventry and I, till noon. Then I took him in to dine with me, I having a wild goose roasted and a cold chine of beef and a barrel of oysters. We dined alone in my chamber, and then he and I to fit ourselfs for horseback, he having brought me a horse; and so to Debtford, the ways being very dirty. There we walked up and down the yard and wet-dock and did our main business, which was to examine the proof of our new way of the Call-bookes, which we think will be of great use.

19. By coach to Mr. Povys, being invited thither by a messenger this morning from him – where really, he made a most excellent and large dinner, even to admiration; he bidding us in a frolique to call for what we had a mind and he would undertake to give it us – and we did, for prawns – Swan – venison after I had thought the dinner was quite done, and he did immediately produce it, which I thought great plenty. And he seems to set off his rest in this plenty and the neatness of his house; which he after dinner showed me from room to room, so beset with delicate pictures, and above all, a piece of per[s]pective in his closet in the low parler. His stable, where was some most delicate horses, and the very racks painted, and mangers, with a neat leaden painted cistern and the walls done with Dutch tiles like my chimnies.

But still, above all things, he bid me go down into his wine-cellar, where upon several shelves there stood bottles of all sorts of wine, new and old, with labells pasted upon each bottle, and in that order and plenty as I never saw books in a bookseller's shop. And herein, I observe, he puts his highest content and will accordingly commend all that he hath, but still they deserve to be so.

February 11.   Took a glister in the morning and rise in the afternoon. My wife and I dined on a pullet and I eat heartily – having eat nothing since Sunday but water-gruel and posset-drink. But must needs say that our new maid Mary hath played her part very well, in her readiness and discretion in attending me, of which I am very glad.

15.   *Lords day*. Sending Will to church, myself stayed at home, hanging up in my green chamber my picture of the *Soveraigne* and putting some things in order there. So to dinner to three Duckes and two Teales, my wife and I. Then to church, where a dull sermon; and so home.

March 19.   Up betimes and to Woolwich all alone by water, where took the officers most a-bed. I walked and enquired how all matters and businesses go. And by and by to the Clerk of the Cheques house and there eat some of his good Jamaica brawne, and so walked to Greenwich – part of the way Deane walking with me, talking of the pride and corruption of most of his fellow officers of the yard (and which I believe to be true). So to Deptford, where I did the same to great content. At noon Mr. Wayth took me to his house, where I dined and saw his wife, a pretty woman, and had a good fish dinner;

and after dinner he and I walked to Redriffe, talking of several errors in the Navy; by which I learned a great deal and was glad of his company. So by water home, and by and by to the office, where we sat till almost 9 at night. So after doing my own business in my office, writing letters &c., home to supper and to bed, being weary and vexed that I do not find other people so willing to do business as myself when I have taken pains to find out what in the yards is wanting and fitting to be done.

April 4.    Up betimes and to my office. Home to dinner whither by and by comes Roger Pepys, Mrs. Turner, her daughter, Joyce Norton and a young lady, a daughter of Coll. Cockes – my uncle Wight – his wife and Mrs. Anne Wight – this being my feast, in lieu of what I should have had a few days ago, for my cutting of the Stone, for which the Lord make me truly thankful. Very merry before, at, and after dinner, and the more for that my dinner was great and most neatly dressed by our own only mayde. We had a Fricasse of rabbets and chicken – a leg of mutton boiled – three carps in a dish – a great dish of a side of lamb – a dish roasted pigeons – a dish of four lobsters – three tarts – a Lampry pie, a most rare pie – a dish of anchoves – good wine of several sorts; and all things mighty noble and to my great content. After dinner to Hide parke. At the parke was the King, and in another coach my Lady Castlemayne, they greeting one another at every Tour. Here about an hour; and so leaving all by the way, we home and find the house as clean as if nothing had been done there today from top to bottom – which made us give the Cooke 12*d*. a piece, each of us.

17. Up by 5 a-clock, as I have long done, and to my office all the morning; at noon home to dinner with my father with us. Our dinner, it being Goodfriday, was only sugar sopps and fish; the only time that we have had a Lenten dinner all this Lent. This morning Mr. Hunt the instrument-maker brought me home a Basse viall to see whether I like it, which I do not very well; besides, I am under a doubt whether I had best buy one yet or no – because of spoiling my present mind and love to business.

July 8. Being weary and going to bed late last night, I slept till 7 a-clock, it raining mighty hard, and so did every minute of the day after, sadly – that I know not what will become of the corn this year, we having had but two fair days these many months. Up and to my office, where all the morning busy. And then at noon home to dinner alone, upon a good dish of eeles given me by Michell the Bewpers-man. And then to my viall a little. And then down into the cellar, and up and down with Mr. Turner to see where his vault for turds may be made bigger, or another made him; which I think may well be. And so to my office, where very busy all day setting things in order, my contract books, and preparing things against the next sitting. In the evening I received letters out of the country; among others, from my wife, who methinks writes so coldly that I am much troubled at it and I fear shall have much ado to bring her to her old good temper. So home to supper and music, which is all the pleasure I have of late given myself or is fit I should others, spending too much time and money. Going in, I stepped to Sir W. Batten and there stayed and talked with him, my Lady being in the country, and sent for some lobsters; and Mrs. Turner came in and did bring us an Umble-pie hot out of her oven, extraordinary good, and afterward some spirits of her making (in which she hath great judgment), very good; and so home, merry with this night's refreshment.

18.   Up and to my office, where all the morning. And Sir J. Mennes and I did a little, and but a little, business at the office. So I eate a bit of victuals at home and so abroad to several places, as my booksellers; and lastly to Westminster hall – where I expected some bands made me by Mrs. Lane. By and by Mrs. Lane comes; and my bands not being done, she and I parted and met at the Crowne in the palace yard, where we eat (a chicken I sent for) and drank and were mighty merry, and I had my full liberty of towsing her and doing what I would but the last thing of all.

24.   To Mr. Blands, where Mr. Povey, Gauden and I were invited to dinner – which we had very finely, and great plenty but for drink, though many and good; I drunk nothing but small beer and water, which I drunk so much that I wish it may not do me hurt.

October 6.   Slept pretty well, and my wife waked to ring the bell to call up our maids to the washing about 4 a-clock and I was, and she, angry that our bell did not wake them sooner; but I will get a bigger bell. So we to sleep again till 8 a-clock. At noon, Lewellin coming to me, I took him and Deane, and there met my uncle Thomas and we dined together. But was vexed that it being washing-day, we had no meat dressed; but sent to the cook's and my people had so little wit to send in our meat from abroad in the cook's dishes, which were marked with the name of the Cooke upon them; by which, if they observed anything, they might know it was not my own dinner. Finding myself beginning to be troubled with wind, as I used to be, and with pain in making water, [at night] I took a couple of pills that I had by me of Mr. Hollyards.

13.   *Rules for my health*. I. To begin to keep myself warm as I can. 2. Strain as little as ever I can backwards, remembering that my pain will come by and by, though in the very straining I do not feel it. 3. Either by physic forward or by clyster backward, or both ways, to get an easy and plentiful going to stool and breaking of wind. 4. To begin to suspect my health immediately when I begin to become costive and bound, and by all means to keep my body loose, and that to obtain presently after I find myself going to the contrary.

29.   Up, it being *my Lord Mayors Day*, Sir Anthony Bateman. This morning was brought home my new velvet cloak; that is, lined with velvet, a good cloth the outside – the first that ever I had in my life, and I pray God it may not be too soon now that I begin to wear it. I had it this day brought home, thinking to have worn it to dinner; but I thought it would be better to go without it because of the Crowde, and so I did not wear it. In dressing myself and wanting a band, I found all my bands that were newly made clean, so ill-smoothed that I crumpled them and flung them all on the ground and was angry

with Jane, which made the poor girl mighty sad, so that I were troubled for it afterwards. At noon I went forth, and by coach to Guild Hall (by the way calling to shit at Mr. Rawlinsons) and there was admitted; and meeting with Mr. Proby (Sir R. Ford's son) and Lieut.- Coll. Baron, a City commander, we went up and down to see the tables; where under every salt there was a Bill of fare, and at the end of the table the persons proper for that table. Many were the tables, but none in the Hall but the Mayors and the Lords of the privy Councell that had napkins or knives – which was very strange. We went into the Buttry and there stayed and talked, and then into the hall again; and there wine was offered and they drunk, I only drinking some Hypocras, which doth not break my vowe, it being, to the best of my present judgment, only a mixed compound drink, and not any wine – if I am mistaken, God forgive me; but I hope and do think I am not. By and by met with Creed; and we with the others went within the several Courts and there saw the tables prepared for the ladies and Judges and Bishops – all great sign of a great dinner to come. By and by, about one a-clock, before the Lord Mayor came, came into the hall, from the room where they were first led into, the Lord Chancellor (Archbishopp before him), with the Lords of the Council and other Bishopps, and they to dinner. Anon comes the Lord Mayor, who went up to the Lords and then to the other tables to bid wellcome; and so all to dinner. I set near Proby, Baron, and Creed at the Merchant Strangers table – where ten good dishes to a messe, with plenty of wine of all sorts, of which I drunk none; but it was very unpleasing that we had no napkins nor change of trenchers, and drunk out of earthen pitchers and wooden dishes. It happened that, after the Lords had half dined, came the French Ambassador up to the Lords' table, where he was to have sat; but finding the table set, he would not sit down nor dine with the Lord Mayor, who was not yet come, nor have a table to himself, which was offered; but in a discontent went away again. After I had dined, I and Creed rose and went up and down the house, and up to the ladies room and there stayed gazing upon them. But though there were many and fine, both young and old, yet I could not discern one handsome face there, which was very strange. I expected Musique, but there was none; but only trumpets and drums, which displeased me. The dinner, it seems, is made by the Mayor and two Sheriffs for the time being, the Lord Mayor paying one half and they the other – and the whole, Proby says, is reckoned to come to about 7 or 800*l* at most. Being wearied with looking upon a company of ugly women, Creed and I went away; and took coach and through Cheapside and there saw the pageants, which were very silly. And thence to the Temple; where meeting Greatorex, he and we to the Hercules pillers, there to show me the manner of his going about a great work of drayning of Fenns, which I desired much to know; but it did not appear very satisfactory to me as he discoursed it, and I doubt he will fail in it.

November 17. [. . .] So home, Mr. Hollyard being come. I had great discourse with him about my disease. He tells me again that I must eat in a morning some loosening grewell; and at night, roasted apples. That I must drink now and then ale with my wine, and eat bread and butter and honey – and rye bread if I can endure it, it being loosening. I must also take once a week a glister of his past prescription; only, honey now and then instead of butter – which things I am now resolved to apply myself to. He being gone, I to my office again to a little business; and then home to supper and to bed – being in a little pain by drinking of cold small beer today, and being in a cold room at the Taverne I believe.

29. *Lords day*. [. . .] A good dinner we had of *bœuf a la mode*, but not dressed so well as my wife used to do it. So after dinner I to the French church; but that being too far begun, I came back to St. Dunstans by us, and heard a good sermon and so home.

December 11. To the Coffee-house and there, among others, had good discourse with an Iron-merchant, who tells me the great evil of discouraging our natural manufacture of England in that commodity by suffering the Swede to bring in three times more then ever they did, and our own Iron workes be lost – as almost half of them, he says, are already. Then I went and sat by Mr. Harrington and some East Country merchants; and talking of the country about Quinsborough [Königsberg, East Prussia] and thereabouts – he told us himself that for fish, none there, the poorest body, will buy a dead fish; but must be alive, unless it be in winter; and then they told us the manner of putting their nets into the water through holes made in the thicke Ice; they will spread a net of half a mile long, and he hath known 130 and 170 barrells of fish taken at one draught. And then the people comes with Sledges upon the Ice, with snow at the Bottome, and lay the fish in and cover them with snow, and so carry them to market. And he hath seen when the said fish have been frozen in the sled, so as that he hath taken a fish and broke a-pieces, so hard it hath been; and yet the same fishes, taken out of the snow and brought into a hot room, will be alive and leap up and down. Swallow often are brought up in their nets out of the mudd from under water, hanging together to some twigg or other, dead in ropes; and brought to the fire, will come to life. Fowl killed in December (Ald. Barker said) he did buy; and putting into the box under his sled, did forget to take them out to eate till Aprill next, and they then were found there and were, through the frost, as sweet and fresh and eat as well as at first killed. Young Beares are there; their flesh sold in market as ordinarily as beef here, and is excellent sweet meat. They tell us that Beares there do never hurt anybody, but fly away from you unless you pursue and set upon them – but Wolves do much mischief. Mr. Harrington told us how they do to get so much honey as they send abroad. They make hallow a great Firr tree, leaving only a small slitt down straight in one place; and this they close up again, only leave a little hole and there the Bees go in and fill the bodies of these trees as full of wax and honey as they can hold; and the inhabitants at their times go and open that slit and take what they please, without killing the bees, and so let them live there still and make more. Firr trees are always planted close together, because of keeping one another from the violence of the windes; and when a fellet is made, they leave here and there a grown tree to preserve the young ones coming up. The great entertainment and sport of the Duke of Corland and the princes thereabouts is hunting; which is not with dogs as we, but he appoints such a day and summons all the country people as to a *Campagnia*; and by several companies gives every one their circuit, and they agree upon a place where the Toyle is to be set; and so, making fires every company as they go, they drive all the wild beast – whether bears – wolfe, foxes, Swine, and stags and rowes, into the Toyle; and there the great men have their stands in such and such places and shoot at what they have a mind to, and that is their hunting.

12.   We had this morning a great dispute between Mr. Gauden, victualler of the Navy, and Sir J. Lawson and the rest of the Commanders going out against Argier, about their fish and keeping of Lent; which Mr. Gauden so much insists upon to have it observed, as being the only thing that makes up the loss of his dear bargain all the rest of the year.

21.   Being directed by sight of bills upon the walls, did go to Shooe lane to see a Cocke-fighting at a new pit there – a sport I was never at in my life. But Lord, to see the strange variety of people, from Parliament-man (by name Wildes, that was Deputy-governor of the Tower when Robinson was Lord Mayor) to the poorest prentices, bakers, brewers, butchers, draymen, and what not; and all these fellows one with another in swearing, cursing, and betting. I soon had enough of it; and yet I would not but have seen it once, it being strange to observe the nature

of those poor creatures, how they will fight till they drop down dead upon the table and strike after they are ready to give up the ghost – not offering to run away when they are weary or wounded past doing further. Whereas, where a Dunghill brood comes, he will, after a sharp stroke that pricks him, run off the stage, and then they wring off his neck without more ado.

# 1664: Cake for a Wake and a Good Hog's Harslet

January 1.   Went to bed between 4 and 5 in the morning with my mind in good temper of satisfaction – and slept till about 8, that many people came to speak with me. And then, being to dine at my uncle Wights, I went to the Coffee-house (sending my wife by Will) and there stayed talking an hour with Coll. Middleton and others; and among other things, about a very rich widow, young and handsome, of one Sir Nich. Golds, a merchant lately fallen, and of great Courtiers that already look after her. Her husband not dead a week yet. She is reckoned worth 80000*l*. Thence to my Uncle Wights, where Dr. [Burnet] among others dined, and his wife a seeming proud conceited woman; I know not what to make of her. But the Doctors discourse did please me very well about the disease of the Stone; above all things extolling Turpentine, which he told me how it may be taken in pills with great ease. There was brought to table a hot pie made of swan I sent them yesterday, given me by Mr. Howe; but we did not eat any of it. But my wife and I rise from table pretending business, and went to the Dukes house, the first play I have been at these six months, according to my last vowe; and here saw the so much cried-up play of *Henry the* 8*th* – which, though I went with resolution to like it, is so simple a thing, made up of a great many patches, that, besides the shows and processions in it, there is nothing in the world good or well done. Thence, mightily dissatisfied, back at night to my uncle Wights and supped with them; but against my stomach out of the offence the sight of my aunts hands gives me; and ending supper with a mighty laugh (the greatest I have had these many months) at my uncles being out in his grace after meat, we rise and broke up and my wife and I home and to bed – being sleepy since last night.

12.   Up and to the office, where we sat all the morning; and at noon to the Change awhile and so home – getting things against dinner ready. And anon comes my uncle Wight and my aunt with their Cozen Mary and Robert, and by chance my Uncle Tho. Pepys. We had a good dinner, the chief dish a swan roasted, and that excellent meat. At dinner and all day very merry. After dinner to Cards, where till evening; then to the office a little and to cards again with them – and lost half-a-Crowne.

February 11.   Up, and after much pleasant discourse with my wife, and to the office, where we sat all the morning and did much business, and some much to my content, by prevailing against Sir W. Batten for the King's profit. At noon home to dinner my wife and I, hand-to-fist to a very fine pig. This noon Mr. Falconer came and visited my wife and brought her a present, a silver state-cup and cover, value about 3 or 4l. He did not stay dinner with me. I am almost sorry for this present, because I would have reserved him for a place to go in summer a-visiting at Woolwich with my wife.

27.   Up, but weary, and to the office, where we sat all the

morning. Before I went to the office there came Bagwell's wife to me to speak for her husband. I liked the woman very well and stroked her under the chin, but could not find in my heart to offer anything uncivil to her, she being I believe a very modest woman. At noon with Mr. Coventry to the affrican house, and to my Lord Peterborough's business again; and then to dinner, where before dinner we had the best oysters I have seen this year, and I think as good in all respects as ever I eat in my life. I eat a great many.

March 10.   Up and to the office, where all the morning doing business. And at noon to the Change and there very busy; and so home to dinner with my wife to a good hog's harslet, a piece of meat I love but have not eat of I think this seven year.

18.   Up betimes and walked to my brother's, where a great while putting things in order against anon. Then to Madam Turners and eat a breakfast there. And so to Wotton my shoemaker and there got a pair of shoes blacked on the soles, against anon for me. So to my brother's, and to the church and with the grave-maker chose a place for my brother to lie in, just under my mother's pew. But to see how a man's tombes are at the mercy of such a fellow, that for 6d. he would (as his own words were) 'I will justle them together but I will make room for him' – speaking of the fullness of the middle Isle where he was to lie. And that he would for my father's sake do my brother that is dead all the civility he can; which was to disturb other corps that are not quite rotten to make room for him. And methought his manner

of speaking it was very remarkable – as of a thing that now was in his power to do a man a courtesy or not. At noon my wife, though in pain, comes; but I being forced to go home, she went back with me – where I dressed myself and so did Besse; and so to my brother's again – whither, though invited as the custom is at 1 or 2 a-clock, they came not till 4 or 5. But at last, one after another they came – many more then I bid; and my reckoning that I bid was 120, but I believe there was nearer 150. Their service was six biscuits a-piece and what they pleased of burnt claret – my Cosen Joyce Norton kept the wine and cakes above – and did give out to them that served, who had white gloves given them. But above all, I am beholden to Mrs. Holding, who was most kind and did take mighty pains, not only in getting the house and everything else ready, but this day in going up and down to see the house filled and served, in order to mine and their great content I think – the men setting by themselfs in some rooms, and women by themselfs in others – very close, but yet room enough. Anon to church, walking out into the street to the Conduict and so across the street, and had a very good company along with the Corps. And being come to the grave as above, Dr. Pierson, the minister of the parish, did read the service for buriall and so I saw my poor brother laid into the grave; and so all broke up and I and my wife and Madam Turner and her family to my brother's, and by and by fell to a barrell of oysters, Cake, and cheese of Mr. Honiwoods, with him in his chamber and below – being too merry for so late a sad work; but Lord, to see how the world makes nothing of the memory of a man an hour after he is dead. And endeed, I must blame myself; for though at the sight of him, dead and dying, I had real grief for a while, while he was in my sight, yet presently after and ever since, I have had very little grief endeed for him. By and by, it beginning to be late, I put things in some order in the house and so took my wife and Besse (who hath done me very good service in cleaning and getting ready everything and serving the wine and things today, and is endeed a most excellent good-natured and faithful wench and I love her mightily) by coach home; and so after being at the office to set down this day's work, home to supper and to bed.

April 8.   Up betimes and to the office; and anon it begin to be fair, after a great shower this morning; Sir W. Batten and I by water (calling his son Castle by the way, between whom and I no notice at all of his letter the other day to me) to Deptford; and after a turn in the yard, I went with him to the Almeshouse to see the new building which he with some ambition is building of there, during his being Maister of Trinity house [. . .] So home to dinner, and had an excellent Good friday dinner of pease porridge – and apple pie. So to the office all the afternoon, preparing a new book for my contracts. And this afternoon came home the office globes, done to my great content. In the evening, a little to visit Sir W. Pen, who hath a feeling this day or two of his old pain. Then to walk in the garden with my wife, and so to my office a while, and then home to the only Lenten supper I have had of wiggs and ale.

June 11.   Up and to the office, where we sat all the morning – where some discourse aris from Sir G. Carteret and Mr. Coventry which gives me occasion to think that something like a war is expected now indeed. Mr. Creed dined with me; and thence after dinner by coach with my wife, only to take the ayre, it being very warm and pleasant, to Bowe and old Ford and thence to Hackny; there light and played at shuffleboard, eat cream and good cherries; and so with good refreshment home. There to my office, vexed with Capt. Taylor about the delay of carrying down the ship hired by me for Tanger. And late, about that and other things, at the office. So home to supper and to bed.

15–16.   Up and by appointment with Capt. Witham (the Captain that brought the news of the disaster at Tanger where my Lord Tiviott was slain) and Mr. Tooker to Beares Quay and there saw, and more afterward at the several Granarys, several parcels of Oates. And strange it is to hear how it will heat itself if laid up green and not often turned. We came not to any agreement, but did cheapen several parcels; and thence away, promising to send again to them. And anon at noon comes Mr. Creed by chance, and by and by the three young ladies, and very merry we were with our pasty, very well baked – and a good dish of roasted chickens – pease – lobsters – strawberries. And after dinner to cards; and about 5 a-clock by water down to Greenwich and up to the top of the hill and there played upon the ground at Cards; and so to the Cherry garden and then by water, singing finely, to the Bridge and there landed; and so took boat again and to Somersett house.

July 2.   Up and to the office, where all the morning. At noon to the Change; and there (which is strange) I could

meet with nobody that I could invite home to my venison pasty, but only Mr. Alsop and Mr. Lanyon, whom I
invited last night, and a friend they brought along with
them. So home; and with our venison pasty we had other
good meat and good discourse. After dinner sat close to
discourse about our business of the victualling of the gar-
rison of Tanger – taking their prices of all provisions; and
I do hope to order it so that they, and I also, may get
something by it – which doth much please me, for I hope
I may get nobly and honestly, with profit to the King.

3.    *Lords day*. Up and ready, and all the morning in my
chamber looking over and settling some Brampton businesses. At noon to dinner, where the remains of yesterday's
venison and a couple of brave green geese; which we are
fain to eat alone, because they will not keep – which
troubled us. After dinner, I close to my business; and
before the evening, did end it with great content and my
mind eased by it. Then up and spent the evening walking
with my wife, talking; and it thundering and lightening
mightily all the evening – and this year have had the most
thunder and lightening, they say, of any in man's memory; and so it is it seems in France and everywhere else.
So to prayers and to bed.

26.    All the morning at the office. At noon to Anth. Joyces
to our gossips dinner; I had sent a dozen and a half bottles of wine thither and paid my double share besides,
which is 18s. Very merry we were, and when the women
were merry and ris from table, I above with them, ne'er
a man but I, I begin discourse of my not getting of children and prayed them to give me their opinions and

advice; and they freely and merrily did give me these ten among them. 1. Do not hug my wife too hard nor too much. 2. Eat no late suppers. 3. Drink Juyce of sage. 4. Tent and toast. 5. Wear cool Holland-drawers. 6. Keep stomach warm and back cool. 7. Upon my query whether it was best to do at night or morn, they answered me neither one nor other, but when we have most mind to it. 8. Wife not to go too strait-laced. 9. Myself to drink Mum and sugar. 10. Mrs Ward did give me to change my plat. The 3rd, 4th, 6th, 7th, and 10th they all did seriously declare and lay much stress upon them, as rules fit to be observed indeed, and especially the last: to lie with our heads where our heels do, or at least to make the bed high at feet and low at head. Very merry all, as much as I could be in such sorry company. Great discourse of the fray yesterday in Moorefields, how the Butchers at first did beat the Weavers (between whom there hath been ever an old competition for mastery), but at last the weavers rallied and beat them. At first the butchers knock down all for weavers that had green or blue aprons, till they were fain to pull them off and put them in their breeches. At last, the butchers were fain to pull off their sleeves, that they might not be known, and were soundly beaten out of the field, and some deeply wounded and bruised – till at last the weavers went out tryumphing, calling, 'A hundred pound for a Butcher!' Toward [evening] I to Mr. Reeves to see a Microscope, he having been with me today morning, and there chose one which I will have. Thence back and took up young Mrs. Harman, a pretty-bred and pretty-humored woman, whom I could love well, though not handsome, yet for her person and carriage and black eye. By the way met her husband going for her, and set them both down at home; and so home to my office a while, and so to supper and bed.

September 5.   [. . .] And so I to the Change, where a while, and so home and to dinner, and thither came W. Bowyer and dined with us; but strange to see how he could not endure onyons in sauce to lamb, but was overcome with the sight of it and so was forced to make his dinner of an egg or two. He tells us how Mrs. Lane is undone by her marrying so bad, and desires to speak with me; which I know is wholly to get me to do something for her to get her husband a place which he is in no wise fit for.

# 1665: The Meanest Dinner, in the Meanest Manner, to the Basest Degree

January 1. *Lords day*. Lay long in bed, having been busy late last night. Then up and to my office, where upon ordering my accounts and papers with respect to my understanding my last year's gains and expense. Now this day, I am dividing my expense, to see what my clothes and every perticular hath stood me in; I mean, all the branches of my expense. At noon, a good venison pasty and a turkey to ourselfs, without anybody so much as invited by us – a thing unusual for so small a family of my condition – but we did it and were very merry. After dinner to my office again, where very late alone upon my accounts, but have not brought them to order yet; and very intricate I find it, notwithstanding my care all the year to keep things in as good method as any man can do. Past 11 a-clock, home to supper and to bed.

July 7. Up, and having set my neighbour Mr. Hudson, wine cooper, at work drawing out a tierce of wine for the sending of some of it to my wife – I abroad, only taking notice to what a condition it hath pleased God to bring me, that at this time I have two tierces of claret – two quarter-cask of canary, and a smaller vessel of sack – a vessel of tent, another of Malaga, and another of white wine, all in my wine-cellar together – which I believe none of my friends of my name now alive ever had of his own at one time.

13.    Lay long, being sleepy; and then up to the office, my Lord Brunker (after his sickness) being come to the office, and did what business there was; and so I by water, at night late, to Sir G. Carterets. But there being no oares to carry me, I was fain to call a Sculler that had a gentleman already in it; and he proved a man of love to Musique and he and I sung together the way down – with great pleasure, and an accident extraordinary to be met with. There came to Dinner, they having dined, but my Lady caused something to be brought for me and I dined well, and mighty merry, especially my Lady Slany and I about eating of Creame and brown bread – which she loves as much as I. Thence, after long discourse with them and my Lady alone, I and wife, who by agreement met me here, took leave; and I saw my wife a little way down (it troubling me that this absence makes us a little strange instead of more fond) and so parted, and I home to some letters and then home to bed. Above 700 dead of the plague this week.

September 13.    Up, and walked to Greenwich, taking pleasure to walk with my minute wach in my hand, by which I am now come to see the distances of my way from Woolwich to Greenwich. And do find myself to come within two minutes constantly to the same place at the end of each quarter of an hour. Here we Rendezvoused at Capt. Cocke's and there eat oysters; and so my Lord Brouncker, Sir J. Mennes and I took the boat; and in my Lord's coach to Sir W. Hickes's, whither by and by my Lady Batten and Sir Wm. comes. It is a good seat – with a fair grove of trees by it, and the remains of a good garden.

But so let to run to ruine, both house and everything in and about it – so ill furnished and miserably looked after, I never did see in all my life. Not so much as a latch to his dining-room door – which saved him nothing, for the wind blowing into the room for want thereof, flung down a great Bowpott that stood upon the side-table, and that fell upon some Venice glasses and did him a crown's worth of hurt. He did give us the meanest dinner – of beef – shoulder and umbles of venison which he takes away from the keeper of the Forest – and a few pigeons; and all in the meanest manner that ever I did see – to the basest degree. After dinner we officers of the Navy stepped aside to read some letters and consider some business, and so in again. I was only pleased at a very fine picture of the Queene Mother – when she was young, by Van Dike; a very good picture and a lovely sweet face.

15.   Up, it being a cold misling morning, and so by water to the office, where very busy upon several businesses. At noon got the messenger, Marlow, to get me a piece of bread and butter and cheese and a bottle of beer and ale, and so I went not out of the office but dined off that, and my boy Tom, but the rest of my clarks went home to dinner. Then to my business again, and by and by sent my waterman to see how Sir W. Warren doth, who is sick, and for which I have reason to be very sorry, he being the friend I have got most by of most friends in England but the King. Who returns me that he is pretty well again, his disease being an ague. I by water to Deptford, thinking to have seen my valentine, but I could not and so come back again – and to the office, where a

little business; and thence with Capt. Cocke and there drank a cup of good drink (which I am fain to allow myself during this plague time, by advice of all and not contrary to my oath, my physician being dead and Chyrurgeon out of the way whose advice I am obliged to take); and so by water home and eat my supper, and so to bed – being in much pain to think what I shall do this winter time; for, go every day to Woolwich I cannot, without endangering my life, and staying from my wife at Greenwich is not handsome.

24. *Lords day*. Waked, and up and drank and then to discourse. And then, being about Grayes and a very calme curious morning – we took our wherry, and to the Fishermen and bought a great deal of fine fish – and to Gravesend to Whites and had part of it dressed. And in the meantime, we to walk about a mile from the town, and so back again. And there, after breakfast, one of our watermen told us he had heard of a bargain of Cloves for us. And we went to a blind alehouse at the further end of the town, to a couple of wretched, dirty seamen, who, poor wretches, had got together about 37 *lb* of Cloves and 10 *lb* of Nuttmeggs. And we bought them of them – the first at 5*s*.-6*d*. per *lb*., and the latter at 4*s*. – and paid them in gold; but Lord, to see how silly these men are in the selling of it, and easily to be persuaded almost to anything – offering a bag to us, to pass as 20 *lb* of cloves which upon weighing proved 25 *lb*. But it would never have been allowed by my conscience to have wronged the poor wretches, who told us how dangerously they had got some and dearly paid for the rest of these goods.

By and by to dinner about 3 a-clock. And then I in the cabin to writing down my journall for these last seven days, to my great content – it having pleased God that in this sad time of the plague, everything else hath conspired to my happiness and pleasure, more for these last three months then in all my life before in so little time. God long preserve it, and make me thankful for it.

December 21.   At the office all the morning. At noon all of us dined at Capt. Cockes at a good chine of beef and other good meat, but being all frost-bitten, was most of it unroast; but very merry, and a good dish of fowl we dressed ourselfs. Mr. Eveling there, in very good humour. All the afternoon till night, pleasant, and then I took my leave of them and to the office, where I wrote my letters, and away home, my head full of business and some trouble for my letting my accounts go so far; but I have made an oath this night for the drinking no wine, &c., on such penalties, till I have passed my account and cleared all. Coming home and going to bed, the boy tells me his sister Daniel hath provided me a supper of little birds, killed by her husband; and I made her sup with me, and after supper were alone a great while and I had the pleasure of her lips – she being a pretty woman, and one whom a great belly becomes as well as ever I saw any. She gone, I to bed. This day I was come to by Mrs. Burrows of Westminster, Lieut. Burrows (lately dead) his widow, a most pretty woman, and my old acquaintance. I had a kiss or two of her, and a most modest woman she is.

# 1666: Preventing the Parmazan from Perishing

January 14.   *Lords day*. Long in bed – till raised by my new Taylor, Mr. Penny; comes and brings me my new velvet coat, very handsome but plain; and a day hence will bring me my Camelott cloak. He gone, I close to my papers to set all in order, and to perform my vow to finish my Journall and other things before I kiss any woman more, or drink any wine, which I must be forced to do tomorrow if I go to Greenwich, as I am invited by Mr. Boreman to hear Mrs. Knipp sing. And I would be glad to go, so as we may be merry. At noon eat the second of the two Cygnets Mr. Sheply sent us for a New Year's gift; and presently to my chamber again, and so to work hard all day about my Tanger accounts.

15.   Busy all the morning in my chamber in my old cloth suit, while my usual one is to my tailor's to mend; which I had at noon again, and an answer to a letter I had sent this morning to Mrs. Pierce to go along with my wife and I down to Greenwich tonight, upon an invitation to Mr. Boreman's to be merry, to dance and sing with Mrs. Knipp. Being dressed and having dined, I took coach and to Mrs. Pierce, to her new house in Covent garden, a very fine place and fine house. Took her thence home to my house, and so by water to Boremans by night – where the greatest disappointment that ever I saw

in my life: much company – a good supper provided, and all come with expectation of excess of mirth; but all blank through the waywardnesse of Mrs. Knipp, who, though she had appointed the night, could not be got to come – not so much as her husband could get her to come; but, which was a pleasant thing in all my anger – I asking him (while we were in expectation what answer one of our many messengers would bring) what he thought, whether she would come or no, he answered that for his part he could not so much as think. By and by we all to supper, which the silly maister of the feast commanded; but what with my being out of humour, and the badness of the meat dressed, I did never eat a worse supper in my life. At last, very late and supper done, she came undressed; but it brought me no mirth at all; only, after all being done, without singing, or very little, and no dancing – Pierce and I to bed together; and he and I very merry to find how little and thin clothes they give us to cover us, so that we were fain to lie in our stockings and drawers and lay all our coats and clothes upon the bed. So to sleep.

March 17.   Up, and to finish my Journall, which I had not sense enough the last night to make an end of – and thence to the office, where very busy all the morning. At noon home to dinner, and presently with my wife out to Hales's, where I am still infinitely pleased with my wife's picture. I paid him 14*l* for it, and 25*s*. for the frame, and I think it not a whit too dear for so good a picture. It is not yet quite finished and dry, so as to be fit to bring home yet. This day I begun to sit, and he will make me,

I think, a very fine picture. He promises it shall be as good as my wife's, and I sit to have it full of shadows, and do almost break my neck looking over my shoulder to make the posture for him to work by. Thence home and to the office; and so home, having a great cold, and so my wife and Mrs. Barbary have very great ones – we are at a loss how we all come by it together. So to bed, drinking butter-ale. This day my W. Hewers comes from Portsmouth – and gives me an instance of another piece of knaveries of Sir W. Penn, who wrote to Commissioner Middleton that it was my negligence the other day he was not acquainted, as the Board directed, with our clerks coming down to the pay. But I need no new arguments to teach me that he is a false rogue to me, and all the world besides.

May 8.    Up and to the office all the morning. At noon dined at home – my wife's cheek bad still. After dinner to the office again; and thither comes Mr. Downing the Anchor-smith, who had given me 50 pieces in gold the last month to speak for him to Sir W. Coventry for his being smith at Deptford. But after I had got it granted him, he finds himself not fit to go on with it, so lets it fall – so hath no benefit of my motion; I therefore in hon-our and conscience took him home, and though much to my grief, did yet willingly and forcibly force him to take it again, the poor man having no mind to have it. How-ever, I made him take it, and away he went; and I glad I had given him so much cause to speak well of me. So to my office again late; and then home to supper to a good lobster with my wife; and then a little to my office again; and so to bed.

June 13.   With Balty to Hales's by coach (it being the seventh day from my making my last oaths, and by them I am at liberty to dispense with any of my oaths every seventh day, after I had for the six days before-going performed all my vows). Here I find my father's picture begun; and so much to my content, that it joys my very heart to think that I should have his picture so well done – who, besides that he is my father, and a man that loves me and hath ever done so – is also at this day one of the most careful and innocent men in the world. Thence with mighty content homeward; and in my way, at the Stockes, did buy a couple of lobsters, and so home to dinner. Where I find my wife and father had dined, and were going out to Hales's to sit there. So Balty and I alone to dinner; and in the middle of my grace, praying for a blessing upon (these his good creatures), my mind fell upon my Lobsters – upon which I cried, 'Cuds zookes!' And Balty looked upon me like a man at a loss what I meant, thinking at first that I meant only that I had said the grace after meat, instead of that before meat; but then I cried, 'What is become of my lobsters?', whereupon he run out of doors to overtake the coach, but could not, and so came back again, and mighty merry at dinner to think of my Surprize.

August 6.   [. . .] I hear also from Mrs. Sarah Daniel that Greenwich is at this time much worse then ever it was, and Deptford too; and she told us that they believed all the town would leave the town and come to London; which is now the receptacle of all the people from all infected places. God preserve us. So by and by to dinner;

and after dinner in comes Mrs. Knepp; and I being at the office, went home to her, and there I sat and talked with her, it being the first time of her being here since her being brought to bed. I very pleasant with her, but perceive my wife hath no great pleasure in her being here, she not being pleased with my kindness here to her. However, we talked and sang, and were very pleasant. By and by comes Mr. Pierce and his wife, the first time she also hath been here since her lying-in (both having been brought to bed of boys, and both of them dead). And here we talked and were pleasant; only, my wife in a chagrin humour, she not being pleased with my kindness to either of them. But by this means we had little pleasure in their visit; however, Knipp and I sang, and then I offered them to carry them home and to take my wife with me, but she would not go: so I with them, leaving my wife in a very ill humour, and very slighting to them, which vexed me. However, I would not be removed from my civility to them, but sent for a coach and went with them; and in our way, Knipp saying that she came out of doors without a dinner to us, I took them to old Fishstreete, to the very house and room where I kept my wedding-dinner, where I never was since; and there I did give them a jole of Salmon and what else was to be had.

14. *Thanksgiving day*. Up, and comes Mr. Foly and his man with a box of great variety of Carpenters and Joyners tooles which I had bespoke, to me, which please me mightily, but I will have more. Then I abroad down to the Old Swan, and there I called and kissed Betty Michell

and would have got her to go with me to Westminster, but I find her a little colder then she used to be methought, which did a little molest me. So I away, not pleased, and to Whitehall, to the chapel, and heard a piece of the Dean of Westminsters sermon and a special good Anthemne before the king after sermon. And then home by coach with Capt. Cocke – who is in pain about his Hemp, of which he says he hath bought great quantities, and would gladly be upon good terms with us for it – wherein I promise to assist him. So we light at the Change, where after a small turn or two, taking no pleasure nowadays to be there, because of answering questions that would be asked there which I cannot answer. So home and dined. And after dinner with my wife and Mercer to the Beare garden, where I have not been I think of many years, and saw some good sport of the bull's tossing of the dogs – one into the very boxes. But it is a very rude and nasty pleasure. We had a great many hectors in the same box with us (and one, very fine, went into the pit and played his dog for a wager, which was a strange sport for a gentleman), where they drank wine, and drank Mercer's health first, which I pledged with my hat off.

September 2.   *Lords day*. Some of our maids sitting up late last night to get things ready against our feast today, Jane called us up, about 3 in the morning, to tell us of a great fire they saw in the City [. . .] So down, with my heart full of trouble, to the Lieutenant of the Tower, who tells me that it begun this morning in the King's bakers house in Pudding lane, and that it hath burned down St. Magnes Church and most part of Fishstreete already.

So I down to the waterside and there got a boat and through the bridge, and there saw a lamentable fire.

3.   About 4 a-clock in the morning, my Lady Batten sent me a cart to carry away all my money and plate and best things to Sir W. Riders at Bednall greene; which I did, riding myself in my nightgown in the Cart; and Lord, to see how the streets and the highways are crowded with people, running and riding and getting of carts at any rate to fetch away thing[s] [. . .] At night, lay down a little upon a quilt of W. Hewer in the office (all my own things being packed up or gone); and after me, my poor wife did the like – we having fed upon the remains of yesterday's dinner, having no fire nor dishes, nor any opportunity of dressing anything.

4.   Up by break of day to get away the remainder of my things, which I did by a lighter at the Iron gate; and my hands so few, that it was the afternoon before we could get them all away. Sir W. Penn and I to Tower street, and there met the fire Burning three or four doors beyond Mr. Howells; whose goods, poor man (his trayes and dishes, Shovells &c., were flung all along Tower street in the kennels, and people working therewith from one end to the other), the fire coming on in that narrow street, on both sides, with infinite fury. Sir W. Batten, not knowing how to remove his wind, did dig a pit in the garden and laid it in there; and I took the opportunity of laying all the papers of my office that I could not otherwise dispose of. And in the evening Sir W. Penn and I did dig another and put our wine in it, and I my parmazan cheese as well as my wine and some other things [. . .]

This night Mrs. Turner (who, poor woman, was re-moving her goods all this day – good goods, into the garden, and knew not how to dispose of them) – and her husband supped with my wife and I at night in the office, upon a shoulder of mutton from the cook's, without any napkin or anything, in a sad manner but were merry. Only, now and then walking into the garden and saw how horridly the sky looks, all on a fire in the night, was enough to put us out of our wits; and endeed it was extremely dreadfull – for it looks just as if it was at us, and the whole heaven on fire.

November 28.   Up, and with Sir W. Penn to Whitehall (setting his Lady and daughter down by the way at a mercer's in the Strand, where they are going to lay out some money); and to Whitehall, where, though it blows hard and rains hard, yet the Duke of York is gone a-hunting. We therefore lost our labour, and so back again – and I by hackney coach to several places to get things ready against dinner, and then home and did the like there, to my great satisfaction; and at noon comes my Lord Hinchingbrooke, Sir Tho. Crew, Mr. John Crew, Mr. Carteret, and Brisband. I had six noble dishes for them, dressed by a man-cook, and commended, as endeed they deserved, for exceedingly well done. We eat with great pleasure, and I enjoyed myself in it with reflections upon the pleasures which I at best can expect, yet not to exceed this – eating in silver plates, and all things mighty rich and handsome about me.

## 1667: Bellyfuls of Milk and the Best of Cheese-cakes

January 4.   Up; and seeing things put in order for a dinner at my house today, I to the office awhile; and about noon home, and there saw all things in good order. Anon comes our company – my Lord Brouncker – Sir W. Penn, his Lady, and Peg and her servant, Mr. Lowder – my Lady Batten – Sir W. Batten being forced to dine at Sir R. Ford's, being invited – Mr. Turner and his wife. Here I had good room for ten, and no more would my table have held well had Sir J. Mennes (who was fallen lame) and his sister and niece and Sir W. Batten come, which was a great content to me to be without them. I did make them all gaze to see themselfs served so nobly in plate; and a neat dinner endeed, though but of seven dishes. Mighty merry I was and made them all – and they mightily pleased. My Lord Brouncker went away after dinner to the Ticket Office, the rest stayed; only my Lady Batten home, her ague-fit coming on her at table. The rest merry, and to cards and then to sing and talk; and at night to sup and then to cards; and last of all, to have a flagon of Ale and apples, drunk out of a wood Cupp as a Christmas draught, made all merry; and they full of admiration at my plate, perticularly my flagons (which endeed are noble); and so late home, all with great mirth and satisfaction to them as I thought, and to myself to see all I have and do so much out-do, for neatness and plenty, anything done by any of them. They gone, I to bed much pleased. And do observe Mr. Lowder to be a pretty gentleman – and I think too good for Peg. And by the way, Peg Penn seems mightily to be kind to me, and I believe by her father's advice, who is also himself so – but I believe not a little troubled to see my plenty; and was much troubled to hear the song I sung – *The new Droll* – it touching him home. So to bed.

March 20.   With Sir W. Batten and J. Mennes to our church to the vestry to be assessed by the late Pole bill, where I am rated at an Esquire; and for my office, all will come to about 50*l* – but not more then I expected, nor so much by a great deal as I ought to be for all my offices – so shall be glad to escape so. Thence by water again to Whitehall, and there up into the House and do hear that news is come now that the enemy doth incline again to a peace; but could hear no perticulars, so do not believe it. Thence to Westminster hall, and there saw Betty Michell and bought a pair of gloves of her, she being fain to keep shop there, her mother being sick and father gathering of the tax. I aime her de todo mi corazon. Thence, my mind wandering all this day upon mauvais amours which yo be merry for. So home by water again, where I find my wife gone abroad; so I to Sir W. Batten to dinner, and had a good dinner of Ling and herring pie, very good meat – best of that kind that ever I had – thus having dined, I by coach to the Temple and there did buy a little book or two; and it is strange how Rycaut's discourse of Turky, which before the fire I was asked but 8s. for, there being all but 22 or thereabouts burnt, I did now offer 20s., and he demands 50s.; and I think I shall give it him, though it be only as a monument of the Fire. So home to the office a little, where I met with a sad letter from my brother, who tells me my mother is declared by the Doctors to be past recovery and that my father is also very ill every hour; so that I fear we shall see a sudden change there – God fit them and us for it. So to Sir W. Penn's, where my wife was, and supped with a little, but yet little, mirth and a bad nasty supper; which makes me not love that family, they do all things so meanly, to make a little bad show upon their backs. Thence home and to bed, very much troubled about my father's and my mother's illness.

May 12.  *Lords day*. Up, and to my chamber to settle some accounts there; and by and by down comes my wife to me in her nightgown; and we begun calmly, that upon having money to lace her gown for second mourning, she would promise to wear white locks no more in my sight; which I, like a severe fool, thinking not enough, begun to except against and made her fly out to very high terms, and cry; and in her heat told me of keeping company with Mrs. Knipp, saying that if I would promise never to see her more (of whom she hath more reason to suspect then I had heretofore of Pembleton), she would never wear white locks more. This vexed me, but I restrained myself from saying anything; but do think never to see this woman; at least, to have her here more. But by and by I did give her money to buy lace, and she promised to wear no more white locks while I lived; and so all very good friends as ever, and I to my business and she to dress herself. Against noon we had a coach ready for us; and she and I to Whitehall, where I went to see whether Sir G. Carteret was at dinner or no, our design being to make a visit there, and I found them sat down, which troubled me, for I would not then go up; but back to the coach to my wife, and she and I homeward again; and in our way bethought ourselfs of going alone, she and I, to a French house to dinner, and so enquired out Monsieur Robins my periwig-maker, who keeps an ordinary, and in an ugly street in Covent garden did find him at the door, and so we in; and in a moment almost have the table covered, and clean glasses, and all in the French manner, and a mess of potage first and then a couple of pigeons *a l'esteuvé*, and then a piece of *bœuf-a-la-mode*, all exceeding well seasoned and to our great liking; at least, it would have been anywhere else but in this bad street and in a periwig-maker's house; but to see the pleasant and ready attendance that we had, and all things so desirous to please and ingenious in the people, did take me mightily – our dinner cost us 6s.; and so my wife and I away and by coach to Islington, it being a fine day, and thence to Sir G. Whitmore's house, where we light and walked over the fields to Kingsland and back again, a walk I think I have not taken these twenty years but puts me in mind of my boy's time, when I boarded at Kingsland and used to shoot with my bow and arrows in these fields.

July 14. *Lords day*. Up, and my wife, a little before 4, and to make us ready; and by and by Mrs. Turner came to us by agreement, and she and I stayed talking below while my wife dressed herself; which vexed me that she was so long about it, keeping us till past 5 a-clock before she was ready. She ready, and taking some bottles of wine and beer and some cold Fowle with us into the Coach, we took coach and four horses which I had provided last night, and so away – a very fine day; and so towards Epsum, talking all the way pleasantly. The country very fine; only, the way very dusty. We got to Epsum by 8 a-clock to the Well, where much company; and there we light and I drank the water; they did not, but do go about and walk a little among the women, but I did drink four pints and had some very good stools by it. Here I met with divers of our town; among others, with several of the tradesmen of our office, but did talk but little with them, it growing hot in the sun; and so we took coach again and to the Towne to the King's Head, where our coachman carried us; and there had an ill room for us to go into, but the best in the house that was not taken up; here we called for drink and bespoke dinner [. . .]

So to our coach, and through Mr. Minnes's wood and looked upon Mr. Eveling's house; and so over the common and through Epsum towne to our Inne, in the way stopping a poor woman with her milk-pail and in one of my gilt Tumblers did drink our bellyfuls of milk, better then any Creame; and so to our Inne and there had a dish of creame, but it was sour and so had no pleasure in it; and so paid our reckoning and took coach, it being about 7 at night, and passed and saw the people walking with their wifes and children to take the ayre; and we set out for home, the sun by and by going down, and we in the cool of the evening all the way with much pleasure

71

home, talking and pleasing ourselfs with the pleasure of this day's work; and Mrs. Turner mightily pleased with my resolution, which I tell her is never to keep a country-house, but to keep a coach and with my wife on the Saturday to go sometimes for a day to this place and then quite to another place; and there is more variety, and as little charge and no trouble, as there is in a country-house.

August 11. *Lords day*. Up by 4 a-clock and ready with Mrs. Turner to take coach before 5; which we did, and set on our Journy and got to the Wells at Barnett by 7 a-clock, and there found many people a-drinking; but the morning is a very cold morning, so as we were very cold all the way in the coach. Here we met Joseph Bate-lier and I talked with him, and here was W. Hewers also and his uncle Steventon. So after drink[ing] three glasses, and the women nothing, we back by coach to Barnett, where to the Red Lyon; where we light and went up into the Great Room and there drank and eat some of the best cheese-cakes that ever I eat in my life; and so took coach again, and W. Hewers on horseback with us, and so to Hatfield to the inn next my Lord Salsbury's house, and there we rested ourselfs and drank and bespoke dinner; and so to church, it being just church-time, and there we find my Lord and my Lady Sands and several fine ladies of the family and a great many handsome faces and gentile persons more in the church, and did hear a most excellent good sermon, which pleased me mightily; and very devout, it being upon the signs of saving grace where it is in a man; and one sign, which held him all this day, was that where that grace was, there is also the grace of prayer; which he did handle very finely. In this church lies the former Lord Salsbury, Cecill, buried in a noble tomb. So the church being done, we to our inn and there dined very well and mighty merry; and as soon as had dined, we walked out into the park, through the fine walk of trees and to the vineyard, and there showed them that; which is in good order, and endeed a place of great delight; which together with our fine walk through the park, was of as much pleasure as could be desired in the world for country pleasure, and good ayre. Being come back, and weary with the walk, for as I made it it was pretty long, being come back to our Inne, there the women had pleasure in putting on some straw hats, which are much worn in this country; and did become them mightily, but especially my wife. So after resting a while, we took coach again and back to Barnett, where W. Hewers took us into his lodging, which is very handsome, and there did treat us very highly with cheesecakes, cream, tarts, and other good things; and then walked into the garden, which was pretty, and there filled my pockets full of Filberts, and so with much pleasure (among other things, I met in this house with a printed book of the life of O. Cromwell, to his honour as a soldier and politician, though as a rebell, the first of that kind that ever I saw, and it is well done) took coach again; and got home with great content, just at day shutting in; and so as soon as home, eat a little, and then to bed with exceeding great content at our day's work.

18. *Lords day*. Up; and being ready, walked up and down into the streets to Creed Church to see it how it is, but I find no alteration there, as they say there was, for my Lord Mayor and Aldermen to come to sermon as they do every Sunday, as they did formerly to Paul's. Walk back home and to our own church, where a dull sermon and our church empty of the best sort of people, they being at their country-houses; and so home, and there dined with me Mr. Turner and his daughter Betty. We had a good haunch of venison, powdered and boiled, and a good dinner and merry.

October 17.  [. . .] Thence to the office – where all the morning busy; and at noon home to dinner, where Mr. John Andrews and his wife came and dined with me, and pretty merry we were; only, I out of humour the greatest part of the dinner, by reason that my people had forgot to get wine ready (I having none in my house, which I cannot say now these almost three years I think, without having two or three sorts), by which we were fain to stay a great while while some could be fetched. When it came, I begun to be merry, and merry we were; but it was an odd, strange thing to observe of Mr. Andrews what a fancy he hath to raw meat, that he eats it with no pleasure unless the blood run about his chops; which it did now, by a leg of mutton that was not above half-boiled; but it seems, at home all his meat is dressed so, and beef and all, and eats it so at nights also. This afternoon my Lord Anglesy tells us that the House of Commons have this morning run into the enquiry in many things; as, the sale of Dunkirke, the dividing of the fleet the last year, the business of the prizes with my Lord Sandwich, and many other things; so that now they begin to fall close upon it and God knows what will be the end of it, but a committee they have chosen to inquire into the miscarriages of the Warr.

## 1668: Curds and Whey Won't Keep Belly-ake at Bay

May 11.   [. . .] I to dinner with Balty and his wife, who is come to town today from Deptford to see us. And after dinner, I out and took a coach and called Mercer, and she and I to the Duke of York's playhouse and there saw *The Tempest*; and between two acts, I went out to Mr. Harris and got him to repeat to me the words of the Echo, while I writ them down, having tried in the play to have wrote them; but when I had done it, having done it without looking upon my paper, I find I could not read the black-lead – but now I have got the words clear; and in going in thither, had the pleasure to see the Actors in their several dresses, especially the seamen and monster, which were very droll. So into the play again. But there happened one thing which vexed me; which is, that the orange-woman did come in the pit and challenge me for twelve oranges which she delivered by my order at a late play at night, to give to some ladies in a box, which was wholly untrue, but yet she swore it to be true; but however, I did deny it and did not pay her, but for quiet did buy 4s. worth of oranges of her – at 6d. a piece. Here I saw first my Lord Ormond since his coming from Ireland, which is now about eight days. After the play done, I took Mercer by water to Spring garden and there with great pleasure walked and eat and drank and sang, making people come about us to hear us, and two little children of one of our neighbours that happened to be there did come into our Arbour and we made them dance prettily. So by water, with great pleasure down to the Bridge, and there landed and took water again on the other side; and so to the Tower, and I saw her home, and myself home to my chamber and by and by to bed.

20. Up and with Coll. Middleton in a new coach he hath made him, very handsome, to Whitehall; where the Duke of York having removed his lodgings for this year to St. James's, we walked thither and there find the Duke of York coming to Whitehall; and so back to the Council chamber, where the Committee of the Navy sat, and here we discoursed several things; but Lord, like fools, so as it was a shame to see things of this importance managed by a Council that understand nothing of them. And among other things, one was about this building of a ship with Hemskirkes secret, to sail a third faster than any other ship; but he hath got Prince Rupart on his side, and by that means I believe will get his conditions made better then he would otherwise, or ought endeed. Having done there, I met with Sir Rd. Browne and he took me to dinner with him to a new tavern above Charing cross, where some Clients of his did give him a good dinner, and good company; among others, one Bovy, a solicitor and lawyer and merchant all together, who hath travelled very much, did talk some things well, but only he is a Sir Positive; but the talk of their travels over the Alps very fine. Thence walked to the King's playhouse and there saw *The Mulbery-Garden* again; and cannot be reconciled to it, but only do find here and there an independent

sentence of wit, and that is all. Here met with Creed and took him to Hales's, and there saw the beginnings of Harris's head which he draws for me and which I do not yet like. So he and I down to the New Exchange and there cheapened ribbands for my wife, and so down to the Wheyhouse and drank some and eat some curds, which did by and by make my belly ake mightily.

June 9.   When came to Oxfd., a very sweet place, paid our guide, 1l 2s. 6d.; barber, 2s. 6d.; book, Stonheng, 4s. To dinner, and then out with my wife and people and landlord; and to him that showed us the schools and library, 10s.; and to him that showed us All Souls College, and Chichly's pictures, 5s. So to see Christ Church with my wife, I seeing several others very fine alone, with W. Hewer, before dinner, and did give the boy that went with me 1s. Strawberries, 1s. 2d. Dinner and servants, 1l0s. 6d. After came home from the schools, I out with the landlord to Brazen Nose College to the butteries, and in the cellar find the hand of the child of Hales. Butler, 2s. Thence with coach and people to Physic Garden, 1s. So to Friar Bacons study: I up and saw it, and give the man 1s. Bottle of sack for landlord, 2s. Oxford mighty fine place; and well seated, and cheap entertainment. At night come to Abington, where had been a fair of custard, and met many people and scholars going home; and there did get some pretty good music, and sang and danced till supper: 5s.

10.   Up, and walked to the Hospitall: very large and fine; and pictures of founders, and the history of the Hospitall; and is said to be worth 700l per annum; and

that Mr. Foly was here lately to see how their lands were settled. And here, in old English, the story of the occasion of it, and a Rebus at the bottom. So did give the poor, which they would not take but in their box, 2s. 6d. So to the inn, and paid the reckoning and servants, 13s. So forth towards Hungerford, led this good way by our landlord, one Heart, a old but very civil and well-spoken man, more than I ever heard of that quality. He gone, we forward; and I vexed at my peoples not minding the way. So came to Hungerford, where very good trouts, eels, and crayfish dinner. A bad mean town. At dinner there, 12s. Thence set out with a guide, who saw us to [Black Heath], and then left us, 3s. 6d. So all over the Plain by the sight of the steeple, the plain high and low, to Salsbury, by night; but before came to the town, I saw a great fortification, and there light, and to it and in it; and find it prodigious, so as to fright me to be in it all alone at that time of night, it being dark. I understand it since to be that that is called Old Sarum. Came to the town, George Inne, where lay in silk bed; and very good diet. To supper, then to bed.

August 22. [. . .] This afternoon, after I was weary in my business of the office, I went forth to the Change, thinking to have spoken with Capt. Cocke, but he was not within. So I home, and took London bridge in my way, walking down Fish street and Gracious street to see how very fine a descent they have now made down the hill, that it is become very easy and pleasant. And going through Leadenhall, it being market-day, I did see a woman ketched that had stolen a shoulder of mutton off of a butcher's stall, and carrying it wrapped up in a cloth in a basket. The jade was surprized, and did not deny it; and the woman so silly that took it as to let her go, only taking the meat.

23.    *Lords day*. Up betimes, my head busy on my great letter, and I did first hang up my new map of Paris in my green room – and changed others in other places. Then to Capt. Cocke's, thinking to have talked more of what he told me yesterday, but he was not within; so back to church and heard a good sermon of Mr. Gifford's at our church, upon 'Seek ye first the Kingdom of Heaven and its righteousness, and all these things shall be added to you.' A very excellent and persuasive, good and moral sermon; showed like a wise man that righteousness is a surer moral way of being rich then sin and villainy. Then home to dinner, where Mr. Pelling, who brought us a hare, which we had at dinner, and W. How.

## 1669: Mightily Magnified Sawce, for Flesh, Fowl or Fish

February 10. Up, and with my wife and W. Hewer; she set us down at Whitehall, where the Duke of York was gone a-hunting; and so after I had done a little business there, I to my wife, and with her to the Plasterer's at Charing cross that casts heads and bodies in plaster, and there I had my whole face done; but I was vexed first to be forced to daub all my face over with Pomatum, but it was pretty to feel how saft and easily it is done on the face, and by and by, by degrees, how hard it becomes, that you cannot break it, and sits so close that you cannot pull it off, and yet so easy that it is as soft as a pillow, so safe is everything where many parts of the body do bear alike. Thus was the mold made; but when it came off, there was little pleasure in it as it looks in the mold, nor any resemblance whatever there will be in the figure when I come to see it cast off – which I am to call for a day or two hence; which I shall long to see. Thence to Hercules Pillars, and there my wife and W. Hewer and I dined. So to Whitehall, where I stayed till the Duke of York came from hunting, which he did by and by; and when dressed, did come out to dinner, and there I waited; and he did tell me that tomorrow was to be the great day that the business of the Navy would be discoursed of before the King and his Caball; and that he must stand on his guard and did design to have had me in readiness by, but upon second thoughts did think it better to let it alone. But they are now upon entering into the Æconimicall part of the Navy. Here he dined, and did mightily magnify his Sawce which he did then eat with everything, and said it was the best universal sauce in the world – it being taught him by the Spanish Imbassador – made of some parsley and a dry toast, beat in a mortar together with vinegar, salt, and a little pepper. He eats it with flesh or fowl or fish. And then he did now mightily commend some new sort of wine lately found out, called Navarr wine; which I tasted, and is I think good wine; but I did like better the notion of the Sawce and by and by did taste it, and liked it mightily. After dinner I did what I went for, which was to get his consent that Balty might hold his muster-maister's place by deputy, in his new imployment which I design for him about the Storekeeper's accounts; which the Duke of York did grant me, and I was mighty glad of it. Thence to the office, and there very busy and did much business till late at night; and so home to supper, and with great pleasure to bed.

24.   Lay long in bed, both being sleepy and my eyes bad, and myself having a great cold, so as I was hardly able to speak; but however, by and by up and to the office; and at noon home with my people to dinner; and then I to the office again and there till the evening, doing of much business; and at night my wife sends for me to W. Hewer's lodging, where I find two most [fine] chambers of